St Helen's Stories

Alun Wyn Bevan

Gomer

This book is dedicated
to all those who played in the white jersey
of Swansea RFC and the white flannels of Glamorgan.
Thanks for the memories.

Published in 2007 by
Gomer Press, Llandysul, Ceredigion SA44 4JL

ISBN 978 1 84323 827 0 (softback)
ISBN 978 1 84323 919 2 (hardback)

This book is published with the financial
support of the Welsh Books Council

Printed and bound in Wales by
Gomer Press, Llandysul, Ceredigion

Contents

Introduction
Memories of St Helen's

Modern-day county cricket at St Helen's.

There have always been those who collect things – stamps, coins, works of art – but none seem as dedicated as those who collect sporting memorabilia. During the early part of the last century, cigarette companies made the decision to publish cards depicting famous footballers, cricketers and rugby players, and those lucky enough to be in possession of such collections now find themselves sitting on a small fortune, such is the demand for such artefacts.

There are others who cannot resist collecting programmes, and anyone who has, tucked away in a drawer, a copy of the match programme for the encounter between Swansea and the All Blacks in 1935, or a souvenir of the night the Harlem Globetrotters played at St Helen's, could profit substantially. Thanks to my father, a pile of such programmes is now filed away in my attic.

But for me, personally, I prefer to 'collect' stadia and sporting venues. To explain. Thanks to my employers, I have been fortunate enough to witness sporting events in some of the most famous sporting arenas in the world. Starting with the Maracanã in Rio de Janeiro, the list encompasses the River Plate Stadium in Buenos Aires, the Olympic Stadia at Moscow, Montreal, Tokyo and Sydney, Eden Park in Auckland, Soccer City Stadium, Soweto (capacity 104,000 for the World Cup Finals 2010), Ellis Park, Newlands, Loftus Versfeld, Madison Square Garden in New York City, Stade de France and the Queen's Park Oval, Port-of-Spain.

During my teenage years every summer followed a predictable pattern. Weather permitting, Alun Tudur, Elis Wyn, Philip Hicks and I would be found at St Helen's in Swansea enjoying the cricket. We would meet up outside Danny (the local butcher's) at 9.30am and be aboard the red double-decker

South Wales Transport bus some ten minutes later. Once we had arrived in Swansea, the walk to the cricket ground took us past the YMCA and the old Swansea General Hospital to our theatre of dreams, namely St Helen's.

A view of the old ground from the Town End.

Here we would watch in awe as Don and Jim weaved their magic, and Parkhouse and Hedges delivered masterclasses with the bat. This is where some of the best fielders in the world plied their craft: Alan Rees, Allan Watkins, Willie Jones, Jim Pressdee, Billy Slade and of course, Peter Walker.

International cricket at St Helen's: New Zealand v. England, 1973.

If the monthly pilgrimage to the cricket had been something of a ritual, then the annual visit to the Snelling Sevens soon followed suit. The venue for the competition alternated between St Helen's, Rodney Parade and Cardiff Arms Park. The crowds would flock in their thousands to enjoy an action-packed display of rugby football. Along the routes to the ground, supporters could be seen laden down with enough sandwiches (usually spam) to feed a battalion, gallons of Vimto, Kia Ora and Tizer, hundreds of Kunzle cakes, and enough sweets to keep dentists busy for months to come.

It was Christmas 1958 when I received one of my first books dedicated entirely to sport. The book was a present from my neighbours Siôn and Guto and entitled *Crysau Cochion*. Bearing in mind that such a publication printed in the Welsh language was a rarity some fifty years ago, it has become a treasured possession. *Crysau Cochion* was a collection of articles, skillfully and sympathetically edited by Howard Lloyd and published by Llyfrau'r Dryw – it has gone on to become a classic of its genre. One article in particular, written by Jac Elwyn Watkins, the former All Whites player from Abercrave, stands out for me. Jac Elwyn had played for Swansea during the 1920s, had been club captain and played against the All Blacks in 1924. After retiring from the game, he became a broadcaster, appearing as a pundit on the Welsh Home Service every Saturday night, reporting on the day's matches.

Jac Elwyn's piece in the book was aimed at reminding the reader of the history, tradition and magic that is St Helen's. He tells of the first time that he heard the name 'St Helen's' mentioned at home in the upper reaches of the Swansea Valley. The year was 1905 and, although still a young lad, Jac Elwyn was still old enough to sense that his father was in a heightened state of excitement as he hurried to finish his breakfast. He then proceeded to rush off to catch the train from Ystalyfera to St Thomas where the railway line ended near the town's docks. As his father was about to leave, the young lad enquired of his father, 'What's so special about St Helen's?' The reply was a little unexpected. 'You wouldn't understand if I told you.' Somewhat taken aback, the youngster turned to his mother who then explained that Mr Watkins senior was going to watch Swansea take on the New Zealand All Blacks. Ironically, some twenty years later, Jac Elwyn's father would make the same journey, but this time it was to watch his son play against the 1924/25 All Blacks!

The 1905 encounter played before a crowd of some 20,000 had been a close one with the visitors winning by a dropped goal to a solitary try from the home team. Things were, however, a great deal different in 1924 when Swansea (with Jac Elwyn playing on the wing) were thrashed by 39 points to 3.

Over the years, events at St Helen's have in the main given immense pleasure to hundreds of thousands of supporters. The loss against Cliff Porter's New Zealand All Blacks in 1924 was one of the low points, but that is the nature of sport. The ground itself stands separated on the one side by a road, and what was once the tracks of the oldest railway in Wales, from the lapping waters of Swansea Bay. To the west lies the village of Mumbles and the

An aerial view of St Helen's showing the tracks of the oldest railway in Wales.

campus of the University of Wales, Swansea. To the east and in the direction of the town stands the clock tower of the Brangwyn Hall and the stone ramparts of Swansea jail.

Rugby has been played on this ground as far back as anyone can remember, as early certainly as any other ground in the world. It also accommodates first-class cricket during the summer months. Where once there was only sand dunes, in 1870 a decision was made to level the ground. After several years and months of hard work and careful planning, the area was transformed and ready to play host to a long list of sports stars and the thousands of supporters who came along in awe to watch them.

Again in his article in *Crysau Cochion*, Jac Elwyn Watkins lists some of the world famous sportsmen who have graced the turf at St Helen's: W.J. Bancroft, Dickie Owen, Billy Trew, Joe Rees, Watcyn Thomas, Cliff Jones, Rowe Harding, Claude Davey, W.T.H. Davies, Haydn Tanner, Albert Jenkins, Wilfred Wooller, W.J. Wallace, Dave Gallaher, C.E. Seeling, George Nepia, Prince Obolensky, Benny Osler, Gwyn Nichols, R.T. Gabe, Dai and Emrys Davies, Gilbert Parkhouse, Maurice Turnbull, J.C. Clay, Maurice Tate, Don Bradman, W.J. O'Reilly, Harold Larwood, Wally Hammond and so on. And that was only up until 1958!

My personal memories cover a period of some fifty years. My father, although a fanatical rugby fan, was no conventional supporter. It was his practice every Saturday morning to scan the pages of *The Western Mail*, and then, having decided which game took his fancy, announce where we would end up in the afternoon. He preferred to watch an exciting talent or an adventurous team as opposed to following the fortunes of a specific club.

This was one of the reasons why my mother became so well acquainted with the shops in Cardiff, Llanelli, Newport and Swansea. There was an extra bonus during the international period when this retail experience was extended to Princes Street, rue du Faubourg St Honore, Grafton Street and Knightsbridge (she was, however, not quite as animated if the car journey ended at Maesteg, Pontypridd and Ebbw Vale – the shops here not being quite as glitzy!)

Alan Prosser Harries, Teifion Williams, John Hopkins, Jim Clifford – just some of the familiar names I grew up with as a youngster, not forgetting the local boy R.C.C. Thomas or Clem as he was affectionately known to us locals. His father 'Dai John the Butcher' owned the village slaughterhouse. Clem always wore the number 16 shirt on his back when he played for the All Whites. This was because, for reasons best known to themselves, the club officials refused to allow anyone to wear a number 13 shirt. Those were the days when the full back wore 1, the scrum half wore 7 and the hooker sported a shirt with the number 9 on his back.

The All Whites matches, the Snelling Sevens, WRU Trial matches (Reds v. Whites, Possibles v. Probables), Glamorgan Cricket Club against Australia, the West Indies, India, Pakistan, New Zealand – all of these contests have been staged at St Helen's. I have spent many an hour queueing at various booths for tickets, having first parked the car at the recreation ground next to the pitch, or near the Brangwyn Hall or the Patti Pavilion. If there was a really big match then the car would have to be squeezed into a tiny space on the steep hill behind the pavilion leading up to Bryn-y-Môr. There would be a mad dash to join the queue which snaked around the perimeter wall near the Cricketers pub, hoping against hope that when we got to the box there would still be tickets available for the grandstand.

Once these were secured, there was another sprint up the steep wooden steps to our seats. Had today's rules of health and safety been prevalent at the time, then a nightmare scenario would have presented itself to officials. Here was a structure made entirely of wood, housing thousands of people, half of whom were devotedly smoking cigars, pipes and cigarettes!

If a stand ticket was not available then we had to view the game from the terrace on the opposite side of the ground. This was a difficult enough exercise for an adult, let alone a small boy. Anyone familiar with the topography of the terrain will know that there is at least fifty metres separating the spectators from the nearest touchline. Watching play, therefore, was like looking through a pair of reversed binoculars – me in Swansea and the players in Ilfracombe!

If one of our local lads from the Amman valley happened to be playing 'on permit' for Swansea, then car loads of supporters would make the journey to the ground to support him. For those of you not familiar with the concept, it went something like this. If one of the regular Swansea players was unavailable due to injury, a promising 'rising star' from a team such as Brynaman would be drafted in to play for the bigger club. This could happen on several occasions during a given season without compromising the individual or the local village team – as long as he didn't play more than five games. This meant that he was still a Brynaman player even if he did wear the All White of Swansea. Thus it was that Gareth Thomas of Cwmllynfell, Eurfyl Williams of Brynaman, and Colin Davies of Amman United found themselves running out at St Helen's on a Saturday afternoon.

So, we lads were there on the terraces to support our local hero and not necessarily the Swansea team. Come the half-time whistle, there was a mad rush to get onto the field to emulate our man by practising some passing or kicking manoeuvres, and at the conclusion of play we would sprint on again, this time with autograph books at the ready.

Once the game was over, it was a mad dash home through the huge crowds to report how well Raymond Jones had played at outside half or how, on one occasion, Ken Pugh had won the game singlehandedly for Swansea in the dying minutes at Stradey with a deft dropped goal from a scrummage in the shadow of the Llanelli posts. News such as this spread around the village like wildfire so there would be no need to tune into the BBC Welsh Home Service for the sports report just prior to the epilogue.

Being part of those crowds was a thoroughly thrilling experience. How much more exhilarating it must have beeen to don the white shirt of Swansea or the whites of Glamorgan. I may well be a sentimentalist, but I know that the young men of my generation from Brynaman and the surrounding area would have given anything to do just that.

The author (back row, extreme right) officiating at a Welsh Students' International at St Helen's in 1985.

1
A Brief History of St Helen's

COMPILED BY DR ANDREW HIGNELL
(Hon. Statistician, Historian and Archivist to Glamorgan CCC)

The St Helen's ground at Swansea has several unique features, starting with the fact that it is laid out on a reclaimed sandbank and in places the soil is barely eighteen inches thick. The second feature has been that cricket and rugby have happily co-existed at Swansea for almost 125 years, with the ground staging international cricket, rugby union and rugby league. The western half of the cricket square doubles up as the in-goal of the rugby pitch during the winter, adding to the charm, but many would say that the finest feature of the ground is its maritime position.

County cricket continues
at St Helen's.

From the seats in the pavilion enclosure, there are splendid views across Swansea Bay and the Severn Estuary to the Somerset and Devon coast, as well as the picturesque Mumbles Head. Indeed, this coastal location has made the Swansea ground a popular venue with visiting supporters, as well as touring teams.

The ground takes its name from a convent dedicated to Saint Helen that was built by an order of Augustinian Nuns on the foreshore of Swansea Bay during the Medieval Period. During the sixteenth century, the land and the convent passed to the Herbert family, who in turn sold it to Colonel Llewellyn Morgan, who in 1872 agreed to the sandbanks being levelled to create a recreation ground.

Swansea from Townhill.

By the eighteenth century, Swansea was a thriving port, and the area along the shore of Swansea Bay developed into a popular and desirable residential area. The gentlemen used the foreshore for their healthy recreation and there are records from the 1780s of ball games being staged on Crumlin Burrows to the east of the Tawe as well as to the west on the sands near the St Helen's convent.

A notice in the *Hereford Journal* for May 1785 also suggests that a formal club was in existence in the 1780s, with the newspaper carrying a request that 'gentlemen subscribers are desired to meet at the bathing house early to appoint a steward for the day and a treasurer for the season'. It seems likely that the members of this early club just practised amongst themselves, similar to the modern-day membership of a golf club. By the early nineteenth century, fixtures were secured with teams from Neath, Llanelli and Merthyr, and the club secured the use of part of a field near the former convent. Even so, the departure of leading players, and an outbreak of cholera in the 1840s, presented a few temporary barriers to the growth of cricket in Swansea.

The expansion of the transport network in South Wales, and a further increase in trade at the port of Swansea both acted as catalysts for Swansea Cricket Club from the 1850s onwards. With the increase in trade, and the arrival of more migrants, by 1852 there were enough good players in Swansea for the club to field two teams.

The increase in membership, and the growth of the local economy, meant that the Swansea club had healthier finances, allowing them to hire decent professionals, such as Henry Grace and Alfred Pocock, and by the 1860s Swansea CC had became one of the top sides in South Wales. Amongst its leading members was J.T.D. Llewelyn, the influential squire of Penllergaer. The Old Etonian and Oxford-educated industrialist had a wide range of sporting and political contacts in South Wales and London, and as a result Swansea CC secured fixtures against the MCC. With quite an extensive and impressive fixture list, the only worry for the club was the often poor nature of the wicket.

An increasingly popular sports venue advertises its wares.

The rough state of the wicket led to the dropping of the MCC game, but even so, Llewelyn was able to arrange other exhibition games. In 1866 a XXII of Swansea challenged the United All England Eleven, and in July 1868 a game was staged against an Aboriginal Eleven from Australia. The success of these special fixtures led to plans being set in motion for the club to acquire a larger recreation ground to act as a decent and proper home for the various sporting teams representing Swansea.

In 1872 an approach was made to Colonel Morgan regarding the sandbanks lining the foreshore, and by the end of the year, an agreement was reached for the creation of a new sports field. The sandbanks were levelled, turfed and rolled, and during the summer of 1873, Swansea CC played their first games at their new and permanent home. During the winter months rugby football was also staged at St Helen's, and Col. Morgan's land quickly became established as the town's sporting centre.

Llewelyn continued to give his support to the club, and helped to finance the building of a pavilion and dressing room to serve both the summer and winter games. Through his efforts, St Helen's became one of the best equipped grounds in South Wales, and an indication of this was the staging of a three-day game between a XXII of Swansea and District against a United South of England XI in May 1876, followed in 1878 by a two-day game between the South Wales CC and the Australian tourists.

In 1890 St Helen's staged its first county match as the recently formed Glamorgan CCC played the MCC at Swansea in June. However, the ground might have disappeared by that time had Swansea Town Council been successful in its bid to acquire the land for building in the late 1870s. The threat to the ground had come from the western expansion of the town, and the popularity of the seafront with residents and visitors alike, meant that Colonel Morgan's land adjacent to the Oystermouth Road was viewed as prime land for building.

With the area near the docks and town centre becoming increasingly congested, Swansea Town Council passed a resolution in 1879 to acquire the sports field for building purposes. The leading members of the cricket and football clubs voiced their vehement opposition, whilst J.T.D. Llewelyn offered to donate £500 to preserve the field for recreational pursuits. The strong pressure and Llewelyn's gentle persuasion forced the Council to agree that St Helen's should remain as a sports ground.

J.T.D. Llewelyn had also been a prime mover behind the formation of Glamorgan County Cricket Club in July 1888, and through his influence the St Helen's ground staged some of the county's home games. Glamorgan paid their first visit to Swansea in June 1890 for a match with the MCC, and the ground's first inter-county fixture followed in August 1891 against Devon, although the weather badly interfered with the contest.

Since the early 1880s there had been a small groundsman's cottage in the south-west corner of the ground, and by the turn of the century, it was the home of Billy Bancroft, the Swansea and Glamorgan cricket professional and international rugby player, who acted as St Helen's first caretaker-cum-groundsman.

During the early twentieth century, J.T.D. Llewelyn financed a number of improvements to the St Helen's ground, including a £1,200 donation towards the laying of grass banking around the ground, the construction of decent seating and a perimeter wall.

The two-storey pavilion, extended in 1926/27.

After the Great War, a new cricket pavilion was built on Bryn Road, whilst a rugby grandstand was erected along the Mumbles Road in the 1920s. By this time Glamorgan had become a first-class side, and on May 28, 1921, St Helen's staged its first County Championship match as Glamorgan played Leicestershire. The visitors won by 20 runs, and it wasn't until the end of July that Glamorgan were able to celebrate their first victory at Swansea, defeating Worcestershire by an innings and 53 runs.

But victories were few and far between at Swansea in these early years, as visting players often cruelly exposed the frailty of Glamorgan's batting and bowling attack. By the late 1920s the county secured the services of several professional bowlers who could utilise the slow, sandy wicket, and in 1927 Jack Mercer and Frank Ryan bowled Nottinghamshire out for 61 to stop the visitors from winning the Championship. Indeed, there are stories of the visting players sitting in front of the dressing rooms and on the grass bank leading up from the pitch, with tears streaming down their cheeks as they saw the title slip from their grasp.

The two-storey pavilion had been extended in the winter of 1926/27. On the lower floors were the changing rooms, umpires room and groundsman store, whilst on the upper floor was a bar, colonade and veranda. In 1939 this impressive building became the property of the Swansea Town Corporation as the Cricket and Football Club sold the ground to the town authorities, who have been the owners ever since

The St Helen's ground had been staging Welsh rugby internationals since December 1882, but by the end of the Second World War, there were doubts over the future of such games at St Helen's as the Welsh Rugby Union considered creating a purpose-built national stadium, possibly in Cardiff, which would have a larger seating capacity than the Swansea ground.

5

In a bid to keep the rugby internationals, the Corporation made further ground improvements with the grass banking being replaced by tiered concrete terraces, and the creation of the walkway with 67 steps down to the cricket field. These improvements further increased the capacity of St Helen's, and in 1948, 50,000 people teemed into the Swansea ground for the one-and-a-half day's play with the Australians. Indeed, these tourist games, often staged over the Bank Holiday periods, saw the ground packed to the rafters, and for the visiting cricketers, the games with Glamorgan have felt like unofficial Test matches against Wales, and in front of what seemed like half of the Welsh population. Indeed, the ground was packed in August 1951 when Glamorgan defeated the South Africans by 64 runs, with Jim McConnon taking 6-27 as the Springboks collapsed from 54-0 to 83 all out.

St Helen's celebrates the defeat of the South Africans in 1951.

The popularity of Glamorgan's tourists games at St Helen's led to its staging two One-Day Internationals. The first was in 1973 when England beat New Zealand by 7 wickets in a Prudential Trophy game, with John Snow taking 4-32 and Dennis Amiss making 100. The second came in 1983 when the Swansea ground was allocated a World Cup fixture between Pakistan and Sri Lanka. It proved to be a high-scoring affair as Pakistan won by 50 runs after rattling up 338-5 with Mohsin Khan, Zaheer Abbas and Javed Miandad all scoring half centuries.

During the 1980s and 1990s, Glamorgan also staged several floodlit games against a Rest of the World XI, taking advantage of the four 140-foot floodlight pylons that had been erected in 1964 so that evening rugby matches could be staged. As a result, the cricket wicket could not be used for the floodlit cricket matches and these exhibition matches against the Rest of the World teams were played on a matting wicket rolled out on the halfway line of the rugby pitch.

Several changes have taken place in the past few years to the rugby-related facilities at the St Helen's ground. It staged its last Welsh Five Nations rugby union international in 1954, but during the 1980s and 1990s, Swansea RFC developed the facilities for playing and hosting club rugby. In 1981 a large extension was made to the pavilion, with new changing rooms, sponsors boxes and a large VIP lounge also being added.

In the winter of 1995/96 the steep concrete terraces together with the scoreboard on the eastern side of the cricket ground were demolished, and then in the winter of 2005/06, the old wooden grandstand along the Mumbles Road was taken down and replaced by a lower, portable unit. By this time, the Ospreys had been formed as one of the regional rugby teams in South Wales. They play their games at the newly created Liberty Stadium to the east of Swansea, whilst the St Helen's ground is still used by the Swansea Rugby Club.

However, the one thing that all of these recent and lavish developments in the brave new world of commercialism cannot change is St Helen's maritime location and its thin sandy soil. The ground may look very different to the days when Billy Bancroft, Harry Creber, Tom Gange and George Clement lovingly looked after the square. But the old adage that wickets fall as the tide comes in still rings true, and it is not just the Glamorgan captains of the past such as Wilf Wooller or Maurice Turnbull who consult the tide tables in Swansea Bay before going out to contest the toss!

The grandstand from Mumbles Road – before demolition!

2
W.J. (Billy) Bancroft

W.J. Bancroft was the Jonny Wilkinson of his time, described in the nineteenth-century press as a 'footballer extraordinaire'. Fast-forward to the present day and you will find several column inches in the newspapers marvelling at the fact that Wilkinson has been given his own key to the campus at Kingston Park so that he can practise his place-kicking well after the rest of the squad has gone home.

While no one doubts the commitment shown by the Newcastle Falcons outside half, this is by no means a new concept. The precedent had been set a century earlier by the equally dedicated Billy Bancroft. However, it has to be noted that the latter's circumstances were somewhat different from his modern-day counterpart, thanks to the fact that his grandfather was the groundsman and general odd-job man at the ground. The Bancroft family was thus allowed to live at St Helen's.

The family home was a thatched cottage situated almost inside the cricket boundary on the field. The young Billy made full use of his freedom and could be seen practising his kicking skills at all hours of the day and sometimes well into the night. Indeed, those travelling regularly along the front on the Mumbles Railway had grown accustomed to seeing the brown-leather Gilbert ball soar into the sky as the train passed the famous ground. Such was the youngster's dedication that even when his grandfather had called it a day, either due to the lateness of the hour or the adverse weather, Billy was still out there kicking at goal.

Bancroft religiously practised kicking balls from all angles of the field, even replacing the corner flag with the ball in order to attempt inswinging goals. His prowess as a place and drop-kicker was unequalled in his lifetime. David Smith and Gareth Williams in *Fields of Praise* express admiration for the Swansea and Wales captain and full-back:

> Cool, dapper and astute, never seeming to hurry, never troubled in fielding high balls, Bancroft was an infuriating opponent who loved to tease lumbering forwards to catch him as he side-stepped (often laterally) out of their annoyed clutches before, on the run, he would kick for touch with heartbreaking accuracy. Bancroft sometimes paid for his tantalizing runs by being roughly handled but it was mostly very rare for this little man, his hair brilliantined and centre-parted, to be ruffled in his role as the Fred Astaire of Welsh rugby.

It is interesting to note that when we speak of sporting icons and venues, the two are inexplicably linked: Hutton and Headingley, Pelé and the Maracanã, Borg (and latterly Federer) with Wimbledon, Michael Jordan and

W.J. Bancroft – every kick perfectly weighted. A perfectionist.

the United Centre at Chicago and Gareth Edwards and the Arms Park to name but a few. What made the Bancroft and St Helen's combination different was the fact that not only did he ply his trade here, it was also his home and while his fellow players had to make the long trek homewards after a match, Bancroft simply crossed the field and was back in the bosom of his family.

Brian Viner's superb book *Ali, Pelé, Lillee and Me* includes a story about Bill Shankly, one often recounted by the Liverpool centre-forward Ian St John. When Liverpool played Manchester United in the 1960s, Shankly liked to motivate his players by gathering them around a Subbuteo pitch, on which there were figures representing all the United players. Starting with the Alex Stepney figure in goal, he would growl 'He can't play!' and put the inch-high Stepney figure in his pocket. He would then go through the team damning and belittling each opponent with a gruff 'He can't play!' until eight of the eleven players were in his pocket. The three left were Bobby Charlton, Denis Law and George Best. Not even Shankly had the nerve to state that they were useless. However, he would conclude by thundering, 'If eleven of you cannae beat three of them, you shouldnae be wearing the Liverpool jersey.' The same analogy could have been made of Swansea RFC in the 1890s – Bancroft and the James brothers being the Charlton, Best and Law of their day.

Let's not forget that W.J. Bancroft was also an extremely talented cricketer – small and wiry but possessing all the required ball skills and a superb sense of timing whilst batting. He was the first professional to play for Glamorgan at cricket, and in his declining years spent much time on his beloved St Helen's ground coaching the young boys. One of his protégés was one of the most graceful batsmen ever to have represented Glamorgan, the masterly Gilbert Parkhouse. When Bancroft was appointed professional in 1895, his contract differed drastically from present day cricketers. Adelina Patti might have received £1,000 for a concert in the early twentieth century but Bancroft's deal amounted to £2 per week over a twenty-week period in the summer months. His association with Glamorgan County Cricket Club ended in 1960 when, at the age of 88, he sat as guardian to the members' enclosure at the entrance to the playing area at his beloved St Helen's. He played 230 games for the county from 1889-1914; in 1903 he scored a career best 207 against Berkshire and in 1889 took 5-20 against Surrey 2nd X1, including a hat-trick.

W.J. Bancroft belongs to that small, but select band that played at St Helen's, Cardiff Arms Park, Lansdowne Road and Inverleith (rugby), and Lord's and the Oval (cricket). In a career spanning several decades, during which there were many highlights, one occurrence stands out above the others. It was during a rugby match played, not at St Helen's, but at the Arms Park on January 7, 1893. This was the first time Wales won the Triple Crown and also the first time they had beaten the old enemy, England, at home.

In the days and weeks leading up to the match there had been a great deal of discussion on the outcome of the game. A large percentage of the press felt that Arthur Gould's team had the edge on their opponents. If they played to

10

their potential then the formidable strength of the English forwards could be overcome. One factor no one had foreseen was the severity of the weather in the days leading up to the game. The temperature had dropped to well below freezing point, and covering the pitch with straw had proved a futile exercise. There was much doubt as to whether the match would go ahead. Everyone, however, had discounted the ingenuity of the groundstaff of the day and even when several tons of coal suddenly appeared, all around questioned what was going on.

A newspaper report on the morning of the match put everything into perspective:

> The phenomenally successful results which attended the experiment by the groundsman with a small fire were reported to the WRU, and it was immediately determined to carry out this idea on a very large scale. From an early hour on Friday morning a large number of men – mostly drawn from the unemployed class – were engaged to lay down and trim more than 500 devils (braziers), extemporised out of buckets pierced with holes and fixed on bricks. Although there was slight snow during the night, the intense heat from the devils softened the ground in a manner far exceeding the most sanguine expectations. When darkness set in, the spectatcle was an exceedingly picturesque one and the field was visited by a large number of football enthusiasts.

The enthusiastic and conscientious team of workers burned the eighteen tons of coal using approximately forty boiler plates under the braziers to spread the heat, and their efforts resulted in the ground being pronounced fit to play after an early morning inspection.

A crowd of 20,000 saw England lead by a goal and a try to nil at half-time, and they seemed quietly confident whilst huddling in midfield munching their oranges at the interval. Within minutes of the restart, England added yet another try but Wales were far from finished and rallied strongly thanks to the determination and skill of their forwards. The opposition seemed to be tiring and looked a little disconcerted when 'Boomer' Nicholl from Llanelli urged his team, in Welsh, to even greater efforts. Wales were inspired by their talented captain, Arthur Gould, who raced over for a quite spectacular try. The Welsh four three-quarter system then combined to set up a score for Norman Biggs from a superb pass from Conway Rees.

It was 9-7 to England and the red rose brigade soon added to their tally when Howard Marshall from Blackheath crossed for his hat-trick, but Wales retaliated with Gould's second try of the afternoon, 'gliding snake-like through the thickest throng'. Inexplicably, Bancroft missed the conversion. It was nip and tuck and with England's lead cut to 11-9, Wales piled on the pressure. With time running out, referee D.S. Morton from Scotland penalised the vistors some thirty yards out near the touchline. The captain instructed Bancroft to place the ball for the crucial goal but the full-back refused point blankly. 'I'm going to drop-kick,' he said. An argument developed – Bancroft did not want a faulty placing by the holder of the ball and stood his ground. After some debate, Gould threw the ball down and furiously stormed off.

Bancroft took it all in his stride. He was oblivious to all around him. He composed himself, dropped the ball and he tells what happens: 'Before the ball had travelled ten yards upon its journey, I shouted to my skipper, now standing in the centre of the field and with his back towards me, "It's there Arthur!"'

Wales had triumphed by 12-11 and went on to win the Triple Crown for the first time in their history.

3
To Barnstaple – by Boat!

'Trains and boats and planes', a Burt Bacharach composition familiar to all those who tuned in to Radio Luxembourg and *Two-Way Family Favourites* during the 1960s. While the melody clearly made for its inclusion in the charts, it was the words that struck a chord with those listeners who were far away from home and were desperate to be reunited with loved ones.

W.J. Bancroft (left) and Emrys Davies congratulate Gilbert Parkhouse on his selection for England v. West Indies at Lord's in June 1950.

This was the era when transport in its various forms was at an exciting stage in its development. Motorways were being built, airports were springing up and the railway systems in most countries (except perhaps in Britain) were spreading out over the countryside. A century or so ago, however, touring sides had no choice as to their mode of transport. International travel was solely by ship, followed by a further journey by rail (usually steam engine). The

13

Springboks or All Blacks of old would spend weeks at sea and then make the final stage of the journey to High Street Station at Swansea in swank Pullman carriages. In their day, these were considered the height of luxury. The players could relax in the plush carriages of the GWR as the train swept along Brunel's tracks, taking in the green countryside on the journey from London via Gloucester to South Wales. Those teams who alighted at Southampton docks also enjoyed spectacular Thomas Hardy landscape as the great steam train chugged its way to Swansea.

In retrospect this was a far cry from the nightmare scenarios experienced nowadays in the gridlock of the M4 at Coryton, Malpas and Port Talbot. Such is the price of progress! However, modern travel does have its advantages. When Alfred Shaw and Arthur Shrewsbury took a party of thirty players to New Zealand on March 8, 1888, the travelling took the best part of three months. Having endured this lengthy journey, they were then expected to participate in no fewer than 53 games. When the tour party eventually arrived home, they had been away from their families for some nine months. Wallace Raeburn relates in his book *The Lions* something of the conditions which prevailed at the time in New Zealand: 'Our footballers started yesterday for Kawakawa and if they ever get there, which is doubtful, they are going to play a match.'

By the 1950s the journey time to the Southern Hemisphere had been drastically reduced. When the British Lions embarked on their tour, they reached their destination in just over three weeks. It was said at the time that some players found it difficult to settle back into a playing and training regime, such was the hospitality enjoyed en route (not much has changed in that respect!). The first rugby player to fly out to the Southern Hemisphere on a tour was the genius from Gowerton, Lewis Jones. Initially, he wasn't selected for the Lions party to tour Australia and New Zealand but was called up following an injury to George Norton. It was not an experience for the faint hearted as the BOAC had to land constantly for refuelling during the long haul flight to the Southern Hemisphere.

Whatever the adventures that may have befallen these players of old, it was as nothing compared with that experienced by W.J. 'Billy' Bancroft's Swansea side during the 1895/96 season. Incidentally, Bancroft led the side for five consecutive seasons, an honour shared only by Billy Trew and a record which stands to the present day. This was a difficult period at St Helen's as most of the promising players were being lured into the professional game with league scouts constantly to be seen in around Swansea.

At that time players would travel to St Helen's by any means possible, whether it was by foot, bicycle, tram or train. Fortunately for them, public transport in those days was fairly efficient so that they were able to turn up on time for a training session or for a match. Those travelling from the upper Swansea valley would use the LMS as far as St Thomas and then hop onto the Mumbles railway which would then deposit them right outside the ground. For an away match to Cardiff, Newport, Gloucester or beyond, the players would meet up at High Street Station from where their journey was made in comparative comfort and safety, and in the main was hassle-free.

As was the norm at the beginning of each new season, a 'friendly' tour had been arranged to Devon and Cornwall. As the first game was to be played ar Barnstaple, it was decided that the players would be given a treat and the journey to North Devon would be made by sea from Swansea docks. The mode of transport was one of Messrs Pockett's pleasure steamers 'The Brighton'. Historians amongst you will know that Barnstaple provided five sailing ships to join the Armada which defeated the Spaniards in 1588, and it was here also that Francis Chichester, the round-the-world yachtsman was born. The town had developed around the woollen industry, the sheep grazing the lush pastures in and around Dartmoor providing excellent quality fleeces. The natural harbour also provided a haven for ships which set sail from here to all corners of the globe.

Anyway, everyone embarking on Swansea's West Country tour congratulated the club secretary on the foresight and adventurous spirit of his arrangements. The party would not have to leave Swansea until late morning and a short, relaxing cruise across the Bristol Channel was something to look forward to and enjoy. There was, however, one dissenting voice – the captain, Billy Bancroft. He was a nervous passenger at the best of times, and a journey by sea, however short, was one to be avoided at all costs as far as he was concerned. He announced that he felt much safer on terra firma than on any of Messrs Pockett's ships and would therefore make his own way to Barnstaple.

Bancroft set off at the crack of dawn to catch the train, with his players still lazing in bed. In hindsight it would have been better if everyone else had followed the captain's example. The weather deteriorated quickly and by early morning it was decidedly inhospitable, with pewter-coloured clouds gathering overhead. What started as a gentle breeze soon developed into a strong wind. The increasing swell in the channel caused the ship's captain to consider delaying the journey, but in the end the anchor was weighed and they were on their way.

Within a very short space of time the crew and passengers knew that they had made the wrong decision. Those passengers who did not spend their time on their knees with ac acute attack of mal de mer were depositing their breakfasts over the side of the ship. They were caught in a force-ten storm with reported winds of over 80mph tossing the ship in every direction possible. This, can I remind you, was in a period prior to the twice-daily shipping forecasts broadcast on BBC Radio 4. To a man, everyone swore that if they survived, they would never set foot on the boating lake at Singleton Park ever again, let alone venture out into the Atlantic Ocean.

When the ship eventually docked at Barnstaple, the All Whites could have quite reasonably been renamed the All Greens. No one could contemplate going to watch a game of rugby let alone take part in one. The only one eager to get out onto the field was the captain. How those players rallied and played the eighty minutes, and came away with a draw, remains a mystery to this very day. Thankfully, they didn't have to fight the Spanish fleet!

After surviving this opening match, the rest of the tour proved to be an easy ride with the All Whites winning all of their games comfortably. Needless to say, the return journey was made by train and the club treasurer had the good grace to compensate each individual for his traumatic experience. As a result of this adventure, over the last 112 years Swansea Rugby Football Club's travelling arrangements have involved trains and planes – but no boats!

4
The James Brothers

No greater accolade is bestowed on a sportsman than the honour of being chosen to represent one's country. Family and friends (who suddenly seem to multiply) bask in the reflected glory that such an event brings. Imagine how much greater is that pride when two (or sometimes more) members of the same family attain such a status.

The England football team benefited greatly from the inclusion of the Charlton brothers, Jack and Bobby. Ireland can boast the Easterbys, Simon and Guy. Here in Wales we have enjoyed the talents of John and Mel Charles, Ivor and Len Allchurch, Terry and Len Davies, Scott and Craig Quinnell, Alan and Eifion Jones and Richard and Paul Moriarty. There have, of course, been other fraternal duos further afield, like Richie and John Benaud, René and Willy Van der Kerkhof, Steve and Mark Waugh, Colin and Stan Meads, and André and Guy Boniface.

Occasionally the celebrations have been threefold, as in the case of the Chappell family when Ian, Greg and Trevor were all included in the Australian test cricket team. One can only imagine how proud the Mohammads must have felt when four sons, namely Hanif, Mushtaq, Sadiq and Wazir, all played in the same Pakistan team. Again Paul, Richard and David Wallace hold a unique record in playing for the Ireland rugby team and then donning the red shirts of the British Lions.

As records go, it is difficult to beat the Williamses of Taff's Well. Gwyn, Brinley, Bleddyn, Lloyd, Vaughan, Cennydd, Elwyn and Tony all, at various times, played for Cardiff. Bleddyn and Lloyd went on to play for the national team with the former also becoming a British Lion (captaining the team on three occasions during the tour of Australia and New Zealand in 1950.)

Nearer home, there are those who still reminisce about the exploits of the James brothers. No, not Frank and Jesse, but Evan and David James, who hailed from the village of Bonymaen, an industrial area to the north-east of Swansea and bordering the docks at St Thomas. If both were playing today, they would undoubtedly be strong contenders to win the TV talent competitions, *The X-Factor* and *Britain's Got Talent*. As well as being gifted rugby players, they were also incredible gymnasts.

Those supporters in the stands and the terraces were treated to some amazing spectacles when these two were on the field. Gymnastic displays, interspersed with rugby moves, had the crowds on the edge of their seats, clamouring for more. As this period pre-dated the mobile-phone camera and web cams, there is no record available of the events taking place at St Helen's. In addition, very little was written about the brothers in the press and there are only one or two grainy black-and-white images of the brothers available.

Brian Davies's portrait of the incomparable James Brothers – rugby players and entertainers.

Evan and David James enjoyed nothing more than clowning around on the rugby field (someone akin to the former Cardiff centre three-quarter, Mark Ring, who would have felt right at home in their company). A typical routine involved walking on ther hands from the corner flag towards the goal posts – a move which had the crowd in raptures.

During this time the population of Swansea totalled some 120,000 and rugby was the focus of the community, bridging every social class. At the heart of it all were the James brothers, who were hailed as heroes by everyone.

When Swansea beat Llanelli in March 1891, 'their tricks with the ball and with their bodies remind[ed] one more of circus performances than of football contests'. Arthur Gould, one of Wales's greatest ever centre three-quarters, and who played with and against them, was a great admirer but in one piece reminds the reader of their abilities as rugby footballers:

> From some reports . . . one might be led to think the Jameses were not a bit like ordinary players, but that they played some marvellous, bewildering sort of game, with conjuring or legerdemain introduced into football. They are not conjurors but they are exceptionally clever pair of halves who . . . have brought half-back play to a state of perfection . . . They never wrangle, they hardly speak on the field, and no matter how much they are knocked about, they go on playing as if they were proof against injury.

Praise by fellow players is praise indeed!

They were, as one reporter stated, 'like squirrels behind the forwards'. An Irish team in the early 1890s, long before video analysis became the norm, were told in no uncertain terms 'Go for the Jameses; never mind whether the varmints have got the ball or not. By the time you reach them, one of 'em's sure to have it'. They were known throughout Britain as 'the Swansea gems' and 'the curly-headed marmosets'.

They played their first game for Swansea in 1889 but unfortunately only represented Wales on a handful of occasions as a result of their involvement with the professional ranks. They apparently played for Broughton Rangers in April 1892 and were offered jobs at £2 per week in Manchester. The Rugby Football Union declared them to be professional players but they were subsequently, upon appeal, reinstated on January 31,1896. David Farmer, in his excellent volume *The All Whites*, takes up the story:

> . . . the whole of Swansea held its breath as it awaited news of the decision. Indeed, there is little doubt that certain unofficial prayer meetings were held throughout Swansea as many eyes turned to the night sky. Whilst some were undoubtedly praying for Heavenly intervention, a more compelling earthly reason for this unusual stargazing could be traced to an item in the Post earlier that week. 'As a service to our readers,' the newspaper confided, 'we have arranged with J.S. Brown, the enterprising Swansea ironmonger, to use his flashlight to announce the decision of the English Union. That 'flashlight'

was, in fact an embryonic searchlight, which was to become familiar to Swansea citizens many years later. Three contingencies were provided for in the code which was published in the paper:

1. If the brothers were reinstated, an upward shining light would revolve in the sky.
2. If the application was refused, a single light would shine upwards.
3. In the event of an adjournment, a double stationary beam would be seen shining upwards.

With the 'whole of Swansea gazing up into the night sky', the light swung around in gay abandon. The James boys were back!

They were unquestionably two of Swansea's finest rugby players and shaped the sporting thoughts and instincts of thousands of supporters in Wales at the time when individuals liked to see the unexpected and appreciated individual artistry. At Swansea they were given the licence to be eccentric and flamboyant. However, as a new century dawned, they crossed Offa's Dyke in an easterly direction for the last time – they re-joined Broughton for a £200 fee, a weekly wage of £2 and jobs as warehousemen. The James's philosophy was a simple one – they didn't want to play it safe and be good. They decided to take a chance and be great.

5
R.M. (Dickie) Owen

On any Friday night, in any rugby club in the country, you will find them – a group of men huddled over their pints of Bass, Brains, Magners and Guinness, deep in animated discussion about some or all aspects of rugby football. Friends have been known to fall out badly over the question of the best ever fullback, prop forward, try, tackle etc. and of course everyone will have an opinion.

This particular Friday evening was a little different from the others in that, for once in my life, I kept quiet and just listened to what was being discussed. The debate centred around the question 'How many world class scrum halves has Wales produced?' (Now if this had appeared on an 'A' level paper in the mid-1960s, I just might have made it to Oxford or Cambridge instead of a Welsh College of Education).

It has to be said that over the years Wales has been a successful breeding ground for top scrum halves. Ever since the first international was played on Mr Richardson's field at Blackheath in 1881, Welsh inside halves have made a name for themselves worldwide. The list of illustrious players is a long one.

The debate that evening continued for over an hour with more and more voices adding their respective contributions. In the end it was agreed that the final list should comprise seven names: Haydn Tanner, Rex Willis, Gareth Edwards, Terry Holmes, Robert Jones, Robert Howley and the present incumbent, Dwayne Peel. Before anyone e-mails or gets in touch to complain, let me add that several other well-known players' names were put forward but for various reasons were rejected. This 'Magnificent Seven' would, therefore, stand, as voted for by the experts from the upper Amman valley.

When things had settled down, I tentatively suggested that another name should have been considered for the list. He was a hitherto forgotten player, who in my opinion, deserved to be recognised as one of the greatest players Wales has produced. Richard Morgan (Dickie) Owen was born in Swansea in 1876, and would later become a boilermaker by profession. As a young boy, he played for Hafod Rovers before joining the All Whites. Here at St Helen's he was one half of a formidable partnership with Richard Jones. Each had an instinctive understanding of the other's play, so much so that they came to be known as 'The Dancing Dicks'.

It was not my aim to demonstrate a superior knowledge to my friends. Indeed, had I not spent hours on planes and in cars with Clive Rowlands (who knows a thing or two about scrum halves and Welsh rugby history), I too would never have heard of the player. Further research amongst the pages of *Fields of Praise*, the Welsh Rugby Union centenary book, yielded more information about Dickie Owen, who represented Wales between 1901 and 1912.

'OK. You have five minutes to convince us why this guy should be on our list!' said the authoritative voice of Mel Morgans (recently retired headmaster) from a corner of the room. So I presented my case!

'Dickie Owen blazed on to the international scene like a shooting star – bringing a new dimension to the role of scrum half. Ever self-effacing, he stressed that his main responsibility in the game was to deliver a fast, accurate pass to his outside half, thus enabling him to set the backs on their way. His greatest strength, however, was his ability to perform the unexpected; no one could read what his next move would be.

'Owen's many achievements included two Triple Crowns, three Grand Slams and 35 Welsh caps. It was he who orchestrated the win against the New Zealand All Blacks at the Arms Park in 1905, after assuming the role of 'coach' when the team congregated on the Thursday before the game. It was also Owen who dictated the tactics on the day and it was he who started the move that led to the only try of the afternoon scored by Teddy Morgan.

'No one up to the present day has quite managed to master the reverse pass in the same way as the Swansea craftsman. He knew exactly where to position himself and knew instinctively where his outside half would be appearing. On that great day and throughout his career, Owen was 'pivot and playmaker, conductor, producer and director.'

Dickie Owen (fifth from left) swoops to tackle a French attacker.

'He may have stood at just 5ft 2ins tall and weighed a little over 9st 10lbs, but Dickie Owen was a fearless competitor. Compared to his All Black counterpart, Dave Gallaher (who was twice his size and who sported a magnificent moustache which only added to his intimidating demeanour), Owen struck a dimunitive figure. Dickie Owen was blue and black at the final whistle in the Wales v. New Zealand match in 1905 and if 'man of the match' accolades had been awarded in those days, then Dickie Owen would have been in contention for the award.'

At the end of the allocated five minutes, another vote was taken. It was an unaninmous decision. Dickie Owen would be included in the list of great Welsh scrum halves. The 'Magnificent Seven' instantly became 'The Elite Eight'.

I'll let Dickie himself have the final word. This is what he wrote in a 1927 article on scrum-half play:

> My advice to a scrum half is to do away with kicking to touch; or, in fact, any kicking at all. That should be left to the stand off . . . who, however, should not forget that the game of football is intended to be played inside, and not outside, the touch lines . . . My idea is that the scrum worker, directly the ball is heeled, should pass direct and as swiftly as possible to the stand off man . . . to run or kick before the opposition is on top of him. To do this . . . a swift and accurate pass should be given from a stooping position . . . If you're going to pass do so at once, and from the very spot where you get the ball. If you decide to run, also do so at once, and keep thinking as you run.

6
Billy Trew

Yehudi Menuhin was only twelve years of age when in 1929 he played Bach and Beethoven with such sensitivity that Albert Einstein, a member of the Berlin audience, was moved to rush backstage exclaiming, 'Now I know there is a God in Heaven!' Concerts by Yehudi Menuhin constantly left audiences mesmerised and this turn of phrase could also be attributed to one of Swansea and Wales's finest rugby players, the incomparable Billy Trew.

William John (Billy) Trew – first cap against England at Gloucester in January 1900.

Drawing by Rebecca Storch

The 1970s was a golden period in the annals of Welsh rugby. Supporters in all corners of the globe were treated to outstanding displays by the national team. Gareth, Gerald, Barry, Mervyn, Phil, Graham and J.J. became household names and were recognised by sports fans everywhere. There were, of course, other periods, when Wales excelled on the rugby field and none more so than in the last decade of the nineteenth century. It was interesting to hear Gareth Edwards admit on the radio programme 'The People's Game' that he knew very little about Arthur 'Monkey' Gould who played for Newport and Wales during this time. However, after researching Gould's playing career, Gareth decided to include him in his team of Welsh greats, 1881-2007.

But what of Billy Trew? Rhys Gabe in 1946 still thought him 'the most complete footballer who ever played for Wales and D.R. Gent wrote that he was 'easily the finest rugby player I ever saw.' Townsend Collins was of the same view stating that Trew possessed 'unfailing judgement' – a quality which was lacking in the make-up of some of the all-time greats.

I too have to admit some ignorance in respect of Billy Trew – that's until I read *Fields of Praise* by David Smith and Gareth Williams, and realised what a genius had graced our rugby fields. He was a firm favourite at St Helen's, a wing three-quarter in the same mould as Gerald Davies and Shane Williams – slight of frame and fleet of foot. His opponents set out to stop him in his tracks, but were never able to make contact with the swerving, sidestepping flyer as he accelerated away – Baron Pierre de Coubertin would have welcomed Trew with open arms at the Paris Olympics in 1900.

The majority of players tend to slow down momentarily as they swerve and sidestep to avoid an opponent, but this was not the case with Trew. His balanced running was done at pace. Given the smallest amount of space, he was away, leaving his opponents in his wake. Some described his running action like that of a tadpole weaving its way through a muddy pool and many of his tries were scored in this fashion. He would lace his way through the opposing defence and, as they lay prostrate on the ground, he would vault over them and squeeze over for the try.

Billy Trew was a boilermaker by profession. This was a gruelling occupation by any standards and especially so during the late nineteenth century. The hours were long and tedious. A typical shift would last for twelve hours, which left hardly any time for recreational activities. Indeed, most men went home so exhausted that, after their meal, they would just collapse into their beds.

Given that these were the working conditions prevalent in the area during this time, it is a miracle that any young man had either the inclination or the stamina to take part in any sporting activities. That he did take part and succeed at the highest level says much about the strength of character of Billy Trew. It was not considered unusual to see Billy (and many of his contemporaries also) arrive at St Helen's straight from work. They would be bathed in perspiration with muddied faces and often hungry (from lack of food in many instances) for the battle ahead. For these young men, the eighty or so minutes they spent running around a rugby field was a welcome release from the rigours of day-to-day life.

The supporters at St Helen's appreciated the sacrifices that these young men made and that is why, when one of their number, usually Billy, produced such electrifying performances on a Saturday afternoon, he was hailed as a superstar. He won 29 caps for Wales between 1900 and 1913, winning his first cap against England at Gloucester in 1900 in a match often described as the dawn of a golden era when, for a period of twelve years, Wales were to be unchallenged masters of the game winning six Triple Crowns and three Grand Slams. One of the guiding lights during this productive period was Billy Trew, who scored a try in the 13-3 victory at Gloucester. He was a genius by any standards. He captained Wales on fourteen occasions, proving himself a shrewd tactician and an inspirational leader. He refused to captain Wales against Ireland at Cardiff Arms Park in 1907 – he withdrew from the team because his Swansea teammate, Fred Scrine, had been suspended by the WRU, 'for using foul language to a referee.' Trew felt the suspension was unwarranted. Out of Trew's 29 international appearances, Wales managed 23 victories.

His three appearances for Swansea in tourist matches also proved memorable and are worth recording. The All Whites lost narrowly to the All Blacks in 1905 – if present scoring values had been in operation, the home side would have triumphed 5-3, Fred Scrine claiming the only try of the afternoon.

A W.J. Bancroft penalty goal and an Edgar Morgan unconverted try defeated the Wallabies, whilst in poor weather conditions D.J. Thomas's try proved crucial in the superb victory over the Springboks.

Date	Opposition	Score	Captain
30/12/1905	New Zealand	3-4	Frank Gordon
26/12/1908	Australia	6-0	Billy Trew
26/12/1912	South Africa	3-0	Billy Trew

To quote Professors David Smith and Gareth Williams:

> So many things were done with such a minimum of fuss that Trew's contribution could be missed, apart from a sudden filigree flashing passage, yet those who played with him, or saw him, give Trew his own place of special fame.

7
Yankee Doodle Dandy!

Over the last century, players from all over the globe have made their way to Glamorgan County Cricket Club and showed off their talents on the sandy turf at St Helen's. Cricketers from England, Holland, the Caribbean Islands, India, Pakistan, Australia, New Zealand, South Africa, Kenya and Zimbabwe have all, at one time or another, arrived by air, sea or train and have worn the daffodil with pride.

What may be less known is that a player from the United States of America also turned out for the county, and he made the journey to Swansea by foot! Frank Ryan was born in Newark, New Jersey on November 14, 1888. There are many similarities between Frank Ryan and that other Frank (Sinatra), who was also born in New Jersey in a small town called Hoboken just across the Hudson from Manhattan in New York City. It is debatable, however, whether there is mention of the former's birth in the state capital building at Trenton in the same way as Sinatra's has been recorded.

When I was a youngster growing up in a coal-mining village in the Amman valley, we always referred to certain individuals in the community as 'characters'. These were people who, because of certain traits, stood out in a crowd – it may have been a certain sense of humour, the daring deeds they accomplished or the ability to sail close to the wind where the law was concerned. Over the years, recalling these people's escapades has given us hours of pleasure and these days we bemoan the fact that such individuals seem to have disappeared from our society.

Frank Ryan was one such character. A very talented cricketer, he spent two seasons at Hampshire before the committee there decided that enough was enough. He became too much of a headache for the administrators and his contract was abruptly terminated. A forthright, charismatic personality, he became as well known for his antics off the field as for his performances on it. He was a frequent visitor to the pubs along the south coast of England, usually accompanied by a bevy of local beauties.

At the time of his dismissal, Ryan was penniless, but believing he would find employment at Gloucestershire, who would possibly welcome his ability with both bat and ball, he decided that he would make the journey west. Because he had no money, he had to walk all the way from Southampton, sleeping rough in isolated barns along the way. Unfortunately for him, when he presented himself at the club in Bristol, he was rejected.

A weaker character might have crumbled, but Ryan, realising the error of his ways, decided to abandon his decadent lifestyle and concentrate on his cricket. The result was that he spent several successful seasons playing in the highly competitive Lancashire League. It was 1921, and Glamorgan County Cricket

Club had just been accepted as full members of the County Championship. Mindful of the fact that there was a huge leap in standards from what they had been used to in the Minor Counties, they were on the lookout for a player who would help lift their profile in this new competition. When the committee heard that Ryan was available they moved quickly to secure his services.

He arrived in time for the start of the 1922 season, having made the journey from Manchester to Swansea on foot. The first couple of seasons proved to be mutually beneficial to both club and player; Ryan determined to concentrate on his cricket, seemingly a reformed character. His first appearance at St Helen's was nothing short of spectacular – Glamorgan were hosts to Northampton and Ryan took 5-77 in the first innings and 6-89 in the second as the home side won comfortably by four wickets.

Slowly but surely, it was not long before the American began to resort to his old ways. This time it was the public houses of South Wales which proved too much of an attraction – he was drawn to them like a bee to a honey pot. Frank Ryan was fortunate that he lived in a different era for he would have made excellent fodder for the tabloid newspapers and the paparazzi. In today's climate he would have occupied column inches on both the front and back pages of the dailies. There was one occasion when Glamorgan were playing Lancashire when Ryan had to spend the night sleeping under the covers! His excuse was that he had lost his way trying to find the team hotel!

Another time, when the team was involved in a match at Cardiff Arms Park, he used the services of a taxi to chauffeur him back from the Midlands. Apparently, he ran on to the pitch shouting 'Frank Ryan never lets you down!' Be that as it may, the club treasurer was not so amused when he received a hefty bill from the taxi firm!

Commentators of the day insisted that Frank Ryan should have played test cricket for England. He certainly had the talent and his career figures of 1013 wickets at an average of 21.04 speak for themselves. However, his reputation as a heavy drinker and a womaniser made him a bit of a loose cannon – and one that the establishment figures of the day did not quite know how to handle. Many of his peers had a great deal of respect for the American – on his day he was one of the best bowlers in the country.

A particularly memorable performance was on August Bank Holiday 1930 at St Helen's when Australia, the best team in the world, were the visitors. Unfazed by his opponents' reputation, Ryan produced some of the best bowling of his cricketing career taking 6 Aussie wickets for 76 runs in the first innings including one memorable scalp on the second morning: D.G. Bradman b Ryan 58.

There were many similarities between the two Franks from New Jersey – the drinking, the socialising, and the women. One went on to become a global superstar, but as far as cricket aficionados are concerned, the only Frank that counted was Frank Ryan. I wonder what would have become of his career if he had met Marilyn Monroe!

8
Haydn Tanner

The random selection of genes which occurs during the reproductive process results in the creation of an individual who will have exceptional characteristics. These may manifest themselves in the form of physical, intellectual or spiritual traits, as exemplified by the likes of Aristotle, Samson, Einstein, Mozart, Helen of Troy, da Vinci and Mandela, to name but a few.

Ireland v. Wales at Ravenhill, Belfast 1949 – Haydn Tanner spots a gap on the blind side.

It would be crass and inappropriate to add to this list someone who excels in the sporting arena. However, if one were to compile a list of such luminaries, the name Haydn Tanner would undoubtedly be an early entry. He plied his craft on the sporting arenas of St Helen's, Swansea and the Arms Park at Cardiff during the 1930s and 1940s. His career at Swansea began while he was still a pupil at Gowerton Grammar School. Scouts for the All Whites had passed many a Saturday morning observing the half-back pairing of Haydn Tanner and W.T.H. (Willie) Davies as they engineered yet another victory for the school team.

Nevertheless, the announcement that these two schoolboys were to be included in the Swansea team to play New Zealand on September 28, 1935 at St Helen's was received with no small amount of shock and disbelief by the press and public alike. Imagine the scenario. The young scrum half standing outside his headmaster's study – his hand shaking visibly as he knocks the door (due no doubt to a mixture of excitement and trepidation). Once inside, he can barely utter the words, 'Please, sir, may I take the afternoon off next week? I'm playing against the All Blacks!'

There is no record of the headmaster's response, but the young Tanner's request was granted. Thus, on a wet and windy autumnal afternoon in front of a crowd of 30,000 partisan supporters, the young, inexperienced All Whites took to the field to face the might of Jack Manchester's All Blacks. Some said it was a scene reminiscent of the gladitorial games in the Colliseum and, as one newspaper headlined, it was 'Lambs to the Slaughter.'

As the game progressed, it became evident that the Swansea pack was able to hold its own against the much heavier opposition. Indeed, their performance enabled Tanner and Davies to dictate the course of the game – the latter managing to create two openings which enabled the giant Claude Davey to score two tries. Despite the conditions, St Helen's was a cauldron of aggression

29

and passion for the duration of and following the end of the game. At the final whistle, the scoreline read: Swansea 11 New Zealand 3.

Some two months later, and still only eighteen years old, Haydn Tanner was selected to play for Wales against the All Blacks at the Arms Park. This time his partner was the mercurial Cliff Jones. In the tradition of the best folk stories, he was again influential as Wales beat New Zealand by 13-12.

Claude Davey (middle row, centre) who captained the Welsh team that defeated the All Blacks in 1935.

Tanner had now attained iconic status – the press and public idolized him in equal measure. What was the secret of his success? Unlike most scrum halves, Tanner was a big man, physically robust and able to withstand the most bone-crunching tackle. He had a fast, accurate service which seemed to compel his partner to run at speed onto the ball. He could read any situation quickly and possessed a lateral vision which opened up several options for the team, whether in an attacking or defensive situation.

In 1938, Haydn Tanner was selected for the British Lions tour to South Africa. This proved to be an unpleasant experience for the young man as he spent virtually the whole tour on the sidelines following a catalogue of injuries. At the end of the Second World War, Tanner joined Cardiff Rugby Football Club. Here again he was a major contributor in one of the most successful periods in the club's history. In his second game against his old club, Swansea, he scored two outstanding tries which resulted in a 13-8 defeat for the All Whites. In his book *Rugger My Life*, the prince of centres, Bleddyn Williams,

30

heaps praise on the scrum half: 'The great Haydn Tanner was a master of scrum half play.' The late Clem Thomas in his much praised volume *The History of the British Lions*, agrees: 'I would have no hesitation in putting him forward as one of the very finest scrum halves of all time.'

Tanner played 25 games in the Welsh jersey and was pivotal in many of the team's victories. If there is one game that typifies his all-round talent, it is that match played against France at Stade Colombes in 1947. The atmosphere was electric with no quarter asked or given. Wales were victorious thanks to a fifty-yard penalty kick from the boot of Bill Tamplin, but it was Tanner who had provided the inspiration for the win.

On this occasion it was his defensive play that came to the fore in an often brutal ecounter. He managed to nullify the threat posed by his French counterpart, Yves Bergougan (himself revered as a god by his adoring French fans). Time and again Tanner would fall on the ball and, time and again, he would be trampled underfoot by the rampaging French forwards. Bergougan left the field in tears but again, as Bleddyn Williams writes in his book, 'There was never any disgrace in being beaten by Haydn Tanner. I never saw him outplayed.'

In 1948, and for the first time in the history of the game, Australia played their final tour match against the Barbarians, and Haydn Tanner was given the honour of leading an illustrious side in an enthralling encounter in front of 50,000 fans at the Arms Park. The Barbarians won by 9-6 and to this day the aficionados enjoy recalling the intricate moves which led to one score. Tanner broke menacingly from the base of the scrum which had formed near the left-hand touchline and fed his half-back partner, Tommy Kemp. He in turn kept the movement going by passing to Bleddyn Williams, who penetrated the defence before releasing Billy Cleaver, who in turn passed back inside to Williams. The centre threw a long pass out to Martin Turner on the wing who seemed in the clear but for an impenetrable Wallabies defence. Just as he was about to score, Turner was tackled, but managed to pass inside to the waiting Haydn Tanner. Tanner, a maestro, who, in his own field, is up there with the greats.

9
Swansea v. New Zealand 1935

What if? If only! How many times and in how many different contexts have these two expressions been uttered? What if 'so and so' had not caught that bus/train/aeroplane then such and such would not have taken place. If only the cat/the dog/the wall could speak then Mrs Jones would know who broke into her home and stole her purse. If only . . .

If only St Helen's could relate its myriad experiences and give up its secrets over the years, it would indeed make for some very interesting reading. Why, the queues outside Waterstones and Borders would equal any of those waiting for a J.K. Rowling publication!

Whoever was chosen to edit such a tome would have a difficult job on their hands, but one chapter would undoubtedly feature: a description of the match which took place on September 28, 1935 when the All Whites took on the formidable All Blacks. In those days the fullback sported a No.1 on his back, and the open-side wing forward was No.15, so the team sheets read as follows:

Swansea All Whites		New Zealand All Blacks
Edryd JONES	1	David SOLOMON
Gwyn GRIFFITHS	2	Nelson BALL
Ron WILLIAMS	3	Mike GILBERT
Claude DAVEY	4	Brushy MITCHELL
Granville DAVIES	5	Pat CAUGHEY
W.T.H. (Willie) DAVIES	6	Eric TINDALL
Haydn TANNER	7	Merv CORNER
George TAYLOR	8	George ADKINS
Don TARR	9	Arthur LAMBOURN
Harry PAYNE	10	C.S. PEPPER
Joe WHITE	11	W.R. COLLINS
Dennis HUNT	12	Ronald KING
Edgar LONG (captain)	13	Jack MANCHESTER (c)
Wilfred HARRIS	14	Jim WYNYARD
Dai WHITE	15	Hugh McLEAN

Referee: F.J. PHILLIPS (Pontarddulais)

To put the game in its historical context it is interesting to note what other newsworthy items were featured in local newspapers in the days leading up to the match.

The opening of a new halt by the GWR at Alltddu near Tregaron makes a total of twenty two stopping places on the Carmarthen Aberystwyth branch line in a distance of just 56 miles ...

C.K. Andrews had the following second-hand cars in stock – a 1933 Wolseley Hornet saloon, a 1928/29 Austin Sixteen saloon and a Douglas motor cycle ...

Benny Sharkey from Newcastle was due to meet Cuthbert Taylor from Merthyr in a 15 three-minute-round contest at the Mannesmann Hall on Monday, October 1st ...

Kellogg's All Bran was, according to the advert, definitely the gentle, natural way to relieve constipation.

The vast majority of readers would have been interested in just one piece of news – an account of the match between Swansea and New Zealand. Every diehard supporter from Bonymaen to Brynaman expected a detailed report on the build-up to the game itself, as well as a post-match analysis, and every reporter, whether it be for a local or national publication, was only too happy to oblige.

The All Blacks just had to turn up . . .

Jack Manchester's team arrived in Swansea on Thursday afternoon, establishing their headquarters at the Metropole Hotel. They were welcomed by the town's dignitaries, including the Mayor, Alderman W.J. Davies and his entourage, as well as Swansea Rugby Football Club officials. On Friday evening the team attended the first performance at The Empire of the Jubilee Year's revue *Hail Prosperity*, with Tom Moss and the twenty Welch Boy Singers – 60 artistes, 1,000 costumes and 28 scenes. The show must have gone on for hours!

Drama of a different kind was being played out in the Swansea RFC committee room. With several key players (Colin Davies and Tom Day among them) injured in the 3-0 defeat to Cardiff, the selectors had to resort to the oft-used policy of recalling former players to help out in a crisis. Edryd Jones was borrowed from the Metropolitan Police to play at full back instead of W.S. Griffiths, and Claude Davey drafted into the centre thanks to a positive response from Sale RFC.

The news that two Gowerton Grammar School sixth-formers were also included in the team led to supporters being divided into two camps. Whilst some applauded the selectors' vision in calling on the services of the two cousins Haydn Tanner and Willie Davies, others saw this as madness in a moment of panic. It was one thing to do well on a school playing field, quite another to perform well against the best rugby team in the world! Fast-forward to the 21st century and Sven's decision to include Theo Walcott in England's football World Cup squad!

Match day dawns!

The weather was dry but overcast with a light breeze blowing in from the sea. All roads led to St Helen's. It was estimated that GWR alone transported some 25,000 supporters in special trains, which ran from as far afield as Brecon, Brynmawr, Milford, Llanelli, Aberystwyth, Newport, Port Talbot and Neath. The LMS followed suit with a half-day excursion from Llandovery, while the normal services from Pontarddulais and Brynaman were full to capacity. The South Wales Transport Bus Company had to duplicate its services on all routes, and all police leave was cancelled with constables on foot and on horseback in and around the ground.

The 45,000 strong crowd was entertained in the hour before kick-off by the Llansamlet Silver Band. Their fine rendition of some old favourites set the tone

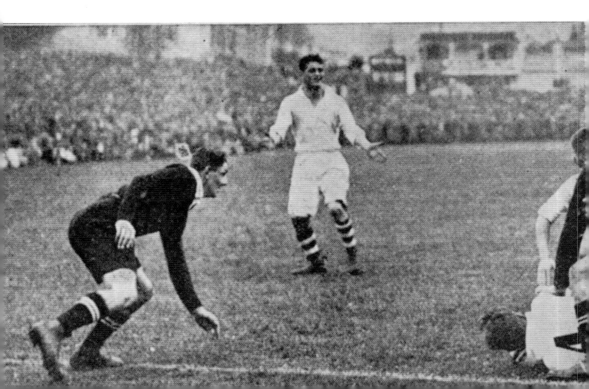

for the afternoon, and the singing, as it filtered through to the dressing rooms, must have sent a shiver down the spine of the most grim-faced forward and inspired the home team to a possible victory. The Swansea XV had been inspired by the occasion long before leaving the changing room and, when everyone present stood and sang *Hen Wlad Fy Nhadau* with pride and enthusiasm, the local doubting Thomases began to believe that a victory was possible.

From the kick-off, Swansea took a stranglehold on proceedings, surprising the opposition with the intensity of their forward play. They competed well and proved from the outset that they had a rock-solid defence. The All Blacks were hesitant, unable to concentrate, and it seemed as if their minds were still focussed on the previous evening's performance of *Hail Prosperity* at The Empire. The first few minutes of a match are crucial to a team's performance, a fact which New Zealand had demonstrated on many an occasion, and on which they built their supremacy. Not on this occasion, however. The All Whites took advantage of a lack of concentration. Their forwards rampaged around the field in total command allowing the schoolboy halfbacks to run riot. After twenty-five minutes play, the Swansea forwards chased the ball downfield towards the Mumbles end, six or seven players took the ball over the try-line for Dennis Hunt to claim an unconverted try. The crowd went mad.

New Zealand responded with wave upon wave of attacking moves, but Swansea were equal to the task. Edryd Jones was rock solid under the high ball, and his spiralling kicks meant that all such attempts were returned to touch with interest. The home side was now rampant. For such a high-profile

Dennis Hunt crosses for the first Swansea try against New Zealand, September 1935.

match, it was inevitable that the national team selectors, 'the Big Five', were in attendance. It could be argued that the whole of the Swansea team deserved to be recognised for their efforts, but the young halfbacks, Tanner and Davies, certainly staked their claim. Amongst the forwards, Joe White, J.E. Harris, Edgar Long and Don Tarr merited some consideration. With the Swansea pack now in full cry, a second try was on the cards – Willie (or should it have been 'Wily') Davies made a glorious break, ghosting through the defence beating three men with ease. Claude Davey was in support and the Welsh international captain raced through for the score. The try was converted by Wilfred Harris. Swansea 8 New Zealand 0.

Again the All Blacks launched another attack and, as a result of some slick passing, Nelson Ball crossed for a try. Gilbert missed the conversion so that the score read Swansea 8 New Zealand 3. A temporary hush descended over the ground as the crowd were silenced and, as if in sympathy with the mood of the spectators, a fine mist descended over the field.

Tanner and Davies's play was just sublime – both players creating havoc in the opposition defence and the outside half's line kicking causing considerable concern for the New Zealand skipper, Jack Manchester, who was forced to contemplate positional changes in his line-up. A third Swansea try followed just before half-time. Again it was Davies who made the running, his run from a line-out had the visitors at sixes and sevens – he passed to Ron Williams who sent Claude Davey in for another magnificent try. Inexplicably, Harris missed a second straightforward conversion. At half-time, Swansea were deservedly ahead by 11-3, but it could and should have been far more.

As the second half got under way, New Zealand launched yet another attack. It looked as if a second try was inevitable. They had reckoned without the courageous actions of Gwyn Griffiths, who pounced on the ball, picked it up one-handed and then in one fluid movement cleared for touch. This proved to be a defining moment in the game.

The All Whites' confidence was now sky high, they felt invincible and this feeling began to ripple around the ground. Amongst a team of heroes, the young schoolboy halfbacks were in a class of their own, their performances belying their tender years.

As the minutes ticked by, the question on everyone's lips was 'Would the team hold out and become the first club team to defeat a touring New Zealand side?' At the final whistle, the whole of St Helen's erupted – the victory was as sweet as it was unexpected. The All Blacks were magnanimous in defeat. In the post-match dinner, Jack Manchester's words reverberated around the rugby-playing world – 'Please don't tell anyone back home that we were beaten by a pair of schoolboys!' During the 1935/36 tour, New Zealand had played 30 matches and lost just three – one against England, one against Wales and one against Swansea!

10
Yes . . . Tennis at St Helen's!

Down the years, St Helen's has played host to a long and varied series of events – from the annual fireworks display to the live transmissions of *Jeux Sans Frontières* (or *It's a Knockout*) hosted by Eddie Waring and Stuart Hall. Billy Graham, the American evangelist, has even delivered a sermon while standing on the halfway line and then there was the circus. When I say 'circus', I don't mean Chipperfields, Fosters, Billy Smart, Bertram Mills or the Moscow State Circus – no, these were staged on the neighbouring Recreational Ground. The circus in question was the Professional Tennis Circus which toured Europe and the United States during the latter part of the 1930s. Between June 7 and 9, 1939, St Helen's was transformed into a mini-version of Wimbledon. A wooden court was erected close to the halfway line, with the players serving towards either the grandstand or the terraced row of houses on Bryn-y-Môr Road.

Over the decades, the Swansea ground has welcomed a roll of sporting superstars: Bradman, Barnes, Bancroft, Bennett, Butcher, Bedi, Botham . . . and Budge. Yes, Budge. John Donald Budge. According to tennis experts, the man from Oakfield, California was one of the best tennis players ever, and it was he who perfected the backhand – unquestionably, it was the finest backhand of all time, almost always an attacking shot, even when on the run.

Budge is one of only five tennis players to have won all the Grand Slam events in a calendar year. He beat John Bromwich (in three sets) to win the Australian title, Roderick Mensel, again in three sets, on the clay courts of Roland Garos, Bunny Austin (in three sets) at Wimbledon, and Gene Mako, in four sets, at Forest Hills. The four others to accomplish this incredible feat are Maureen Connolly (1953), Rod Laver (1962 and 1969), Magaret Court (1970) and Steffi Graf (1988).

We should recall that, at this time, tennis was an amateur sport. After winning those coveted titles in 1938, Budge decided to join a professional tennis circuit touring Europe and the United States. It was the time when sportsmen from many organisations were beginning to be paid for their services and therefore it came as no great surprise when the crème de la crème of the tennis world decided to follow suit. The financial reward from being part of such a body would set them up nicely for the time when they retired from playing.

At the start of 1939, Budge, Fred Perry, Ellsworth Vines, Bill Tilden, Lester Stoefen, Hans Nusslein and others formed part of a group who embarked on a professional circuit. During the summer of that year, the professional game had never seemed healthier. Locally, *The South Wales Evening Post* tennis correspondent was in a state of high excitement at the prospect of such a high-profile event coming to St Helen's. For weeks beforehand, columns would appear in the paper urging everyone to buy tickets and come along to support

37

Donald Budge – the man who perfected the backhand and displayed the stroke at St Helen's in 1939.

such a prestigious event. However, the promoter, Sydney J. Wignall, was rather disappointed with the response – he stressed that 'never in the history of tennis in Wales has such a galaxy of male tennis stars appeared on the court at one time.' Season tickets for the three nights were available at 15s and nightly seats at 7/6d, 5/6d and 3/6d; boys and soldiers in uniform only had to pay 6d. Astonishingly, no provision was made for girls!

When the players arrived at High Street station, they were treated like royalty. The mayor was there to greet them, and a convoy of cars was put at their disposal. The day after their arrival saw Vines and Stoefen enjoying a round of golf at Clyne, while the wives were taken in an open-top car on a tour of the Gower peninsula. According to the *South Wales Evening Post*, 'They were enchanted with the lovely succession of bays, and broad stretches of golden sand.' Vines was delighted that he had beaten Stoefen at Clyne by two holes after giving him a start of nine. Incidentally, he went round in 71, the course par in those days being 74. After an early dinner at the Metropole Hotel, the party was whisked to the Empire Theatre to watch *The Two Mrs Carrolls*.

Throughout the three days, the tennis proved enthralling and Bill Tilden confided, after play concluded, that the final 'had been one of the finest games of tennis he had ever seen.' Donald Budge and Ellsworth Vines slugged it out in front of a respectable crowd who responded enthusiastically to several spectacular rallies, some unbelievable ground-shots and also marvelled whilst witnessing first hand the accuracy of the Budge backhand – the most famous stroke in tennis history. Budge won the contest 9-7, 11-9. The competitors at the Swansea event, Tilden, Vines, Budge and Stoefen were all Wimbledon champions:

The Championship Roll
Men's singles

1930: W.T. Tilden	1937: J.D. Budge
W. Allison	*G. von Cramm*
1932: H.E. Vines	1938: J.D. Budge
H.W. Austin	*H.W. Austin*

Men's Doubles

1934: G.M. Lott and L.R. Stoefen
J. Borotra and J. Brugnon

Unfortunately, the attendance did not come up to expectations and was one of the reasons why professional tennis did not return to St Helen's in Swansea. Tennis followers felt that these contests were mere exhibitions, with players paying for a monetary prize rather than a title. Some questioned the sincerity of the players – were the matches being staged and manipulated, rather than being contested fairly? The Professional Tennis Circus continued for many years with Laver, Rosewall, Hoad, and Gonzales being drawn into its ranks, but the paying public weren't convinced – to them, Budge winning at Wimbledon meant far more than Budge's supremacy at Swansea.

11
Il Buon Gigante played at St Helen's

What if? Those two words once again. What if Llywelyn had been victorious at Cilmeri in 1282 – then everyone living east of Offa's Dyke would be natural Welsh speakers. What if Charles Evans had not been taken ill on May 28, 1953 – then a Welshman would have been the first to set foot on the summit of Everest.

And what if two of Europe's best footballers (Ray Daniel and Trevor Ford) and one of the best players in the world at the time (John Charles) had played in the quarter finals of the World Cup in Sweden in 1958, then maybe Wales would have lifted the Jules Rimet trophy that year. Political decisions led to the omission of Daniel and Ford from the team, but John Charles was forced to withdraw due to the effects of some horrific tackling by the Hungarians in a play-off match, which Wales won 2-1. Subsequently, Dave Bowen's team had to take the field against Brazil at Gothenburg without their talisman, and lost to a solitary Pelé goal, his first in World Cup football.

John Charles was recognised throughout the footballing world as a player of some stature. Indeed, Jack Charlton, one of the heroes of the successful England team of 1966, maintains that he was one of the best players who ever graced a football pitch. Charles's best years were spent playing at Leeds United and at Juventus. A giant on the field, he was also an excellent ambassador off it and everyone who met him agreed that he was a gentleman. Pelé, Puskas, Cruyff, Best, Maradona, Zidane; not one of these illustrious players could overshadow King John – William John Charles.

His early days as an apprentice with Swansea Town saw him endear himself to the staff and fellow players alike. His warm manner, friendly personality and enthusiasm for the game were infectious, and made him a firm favourite at the Vetch. In true fairy-tale fashion, however, it was not at the Vetch that his footballing skills were first recognised. Whilst playing a friendly fixture on a local park,

John Charles leads out his team.

John Charles was spotted by one of the Leeds United scouts who pressed the manager, Major Frank Buckley, to sign him immediately.

So it was that in January 1949, John Charles became a Leeds United player. His signing on fee was £10, and in addition he received a new suit, shirt, tie, shoes and an overcoat. It was not long before Buckley was to be heard boasting Charles's ability in public. 'He is the most complete footballer playing the game today,' he said. Two years of National Service followed in the years between 1950 and 1952, and when he returned to Leeds the boy had developed into a man. John Charles was tall, strong and muscular but gentle by nature. In his book *Cewri'r Bêl-droed yng Nghymru* ('Football Giants in Wales') Geraint Jenkins maintains, 'Although Charles was a giant in strength and stature, he never took advantage of his physical prowess. Retaliation was never a part of his game, for which he gained the utmost respect.'

As a player, he was widely acknowledged to be the finest Welsh footballer since Billy Meredith. He helped Juve to three Serie A Championships and two Italian Cups, and scored 93 goals in 155 league games – an amazing scoring rate against the world's toughest defences. No British player has enjoyed such acclaim on foreign soil. In 38 internationals, he scored 15 goals. One goal, as described by the pundits of the day and those lucky enough to witness it, was out of this world. Wales were playing Northern Ireland at Windsor Park, Belfast and Charles scored a hat-trick, the second goal of which prompted great acclaim. After receiving the ball on the halfway line, he tore through the defence and subsequently fired the ball with venom into the upper right-hand corner of the net, a truly unstoppable shot. 'Unbelievable,' was one headline the following morning.

In his book, *Michael Parkinson on Football*, the writer and broadcaster devotes a whole chapter to the Welsh icon. The title of the piece shows the high esteem in which Parkinson held his hero. He called it, 'John Charles was the best centre-half in the world as well as the best centre-forward.' Physically he was a giant, with the balance of a gymnast and the speed of an Olympic athlete. Bruno Tonioli, a judge on *Celebrity Come Dancing* would surely have approved of his carriage and bearing!

In attack and defence, he reigned supreme and possessed the innate ability of being able to break the heart of the opposition just when they thought they had gained the upper hand. There was no one to rival him when it came to heading the ball, but there was more to this man than just his talents on the football field.

In a career which spanned fifteen years, John Charles's disciplinary conduct was exemplary. His name was never written into the referee's notebook, he was never warned for dissent. He totally ignored those players who set out to intimidate him – he had his own standards of behaviour and stuck to them rigidly throughout his career; a philosophy which stood him in good stead.

An example of John Charles's gentlemanly conduct was witnessed in a local derby played between Juventus and Torino. During an attacking movement, close to the Turin goal, he accidentally floored one of the opposing defenders. Instead of taking advantage and shooting for goal, he kicked the ball towards the touchline and ran towards the injured player. Both sets of supporters looked on in disbelief, unable to comprehend the actions of the gentle giant. You can just imagine what Wenger, Ferguson or Mourhino would have told him!

When John Charles scored his first hat-trick at Leeds, Major Buckley was so impressed that he presented him with three gallons of petrol. The manager was unaware that his player did not, at that stage, own a car!

The Italian public revered John Charles as a god – he was idolised by young and old alike. This was illustrated during the late 1990s when, after undergoing surgery in Italy, he was flown home to Britain in a private jet owned by Juventus Football Club. If any footballer deserved to be honoured with a knighthood, that person was John Charles. Those people in authority who deal with such matters should be ashamed of their lack of action in this quest. Throughout his career, John believed that a footballer never ceases to learn his craft. To quote Daley Thompson, Stewart Binns and Tom Lewis in *The Greatest* – 'John Charles is living proof that sometimes nice guys do finish first. Everything you read about the man, even from opponents, testifies to what a nice man he was, even while playing!'

'Il Buon Gigante' – one of football's greatest sons and he played football at St Helen's – as a youngster with Swansea Schoolboys.

12
1948 and All That!

It's a strange thing, but very little attention has been paid to the extraordinary enthusiasm that these South Walians have for county cricket. The old tradition is that the English own the game entirely, and that it's only they who can appreciate this form of cricket . . . Stuff and nonsense! When Glamorgan came to play at St Helen's, never was seen such enthusiasm. The game went to the South Walians' hearts straightaway . . .

(Translated from Islwyn Williams,
'Y Blaenor', Cap Wil Tomos a Storïau Eraill)

Championship-winning season 1948 : (from the left) Phil Clift, Willie Jones, W.G. Parkhouse, Allan Watkins, Jim Eaglestone, Haydn Davies, Emrys Davies, Wilfred Wooller, Jim Pleass, Stan Trick. (Norman Hever is unfortunately obscured).

On August 24, 1948, Dean Park Bournemouth saw a watershed in the fortunes of Glamorgan Cricket Club. For the first time in its history, the club won the County Championship and it was a proud Wilfred Wooller who held the trophy aloft. It also caused the Fleet Street press to eat their words and to sit up and take note. Rightly or wrongly, the Welsh side had been the subject of ridicule in the newspapers and on the radio – they were regarded as the poor relations. Now they were champions, they could command the respect they deserved.

The games contested at St Helen's played a major part in the Welsh county's success – in fact they won every encounter on the famous old ground. This was thanks in the main to a concerted team effort and the impressive bowling of Stan Trick and Len Muncer. The statistics speak for themselves:

May 22/24/25:
Glamorgan   257 (Clift 57)   227 (Parkhouse 72, Davies 63)
Somerset   249 (Trick 6-77)   98 (Trick 6-29)
Glamorgan won by 137 runs

June 12/14/15:
Glamorgan   189 (Clift 73)   314 (Watkins 93, Davies 92)
Kent   105 (Clift 6-39)   120 (Trick 4-32 Muncer 5-47)
Glamorgan won by 278 runs

June 23/24/25:
Glamorgan   329 (Wooller 80)   187-5 dec. (Davies 75)
Notts   217 (Muncer 5-69)   78 (Muncer 6-13)
Glamorgan won by 221 runs

July 7/8/9:
Sussex   261 (Muncer 8-99)   237 (Muncer 7-102)
Glamorgan   406 (Parkhouse 117)   93-4
Glamorgan won by 6 wickets

Latterly, Tony Lewis and Matthew Maynard's men have shown the same sense of unity and purpose as that demonstrated by the men of 1948. There were no huge egos, no prima donnas in the side. It was truly a team effort, with each member playing for each other. More than that, it seemed that each player was also representing his country, such was the depth of feeling amongst the squad. The constant banter and chatter on the field was echoed by the chanting of 'Waqar is a Welshman' off it. This passion spilt out onto the stands and terraces with the result that the 'Glammy' supporters themselves earned a reputation for their steadfastness even when the team was not playing well. After all, what other county can boast such a following when the team has won only three championships in its entire history?

One of Glamorgan's all-time greats who also became a respected Test Match Umpire – Emrys Davies.

The main character of Islwyn Williams's '*Y Blaenor*', Ifan Harris, is one such stalwart. On his deathbed, he implores his friend to tell him of Emrys Davies's latest exploit:

'Tell me: did – did – Emrys *bach* get his hundred?'
'He did.'
He closed his eyes, and the nurse gestured me to go.

The West Indian wizard (and some time Welshman) Sir Vivian Richards once said that as he led his team out onto the field, or when he walked out to bat, he felt like an ambassador for the underprivileged at home. Everything he did on that field was designed to bring some light, some excitement into their otherwise depressing and dreary lives and to make them feel proud to be West Indians.

This was the same feeling which swept around the ground at Bournemouth in 1948 as *Land of My Fathers* was played over the tannoy and the Welsh dragon flew proudly above the pavilion. The 2007 season has been hugely disappointing for players and fans alike, but we must be patient. The success enjoyed by the club over the last fifteen years has temporarily dried up. While a programme of rebuilding of both ground and team is taking place, it will not, I'm sure, be long before the 'Glammy' faithful will again be in fine voice, adopting every player as a Welshman.

Willie Jones: talented cricketer for Glamorgan and a fine outside half for Gloucester.

13

'This is Alun Williams at St Helen's in Swansea . . .

This is Alun Williams at St Helen's in Swansea . . . Glamorgan are playing Worcestershire . . . Glamorgan have won the toss and have elected to bat.

At the end of the 1940s, the British Broadcasting Corporation embarked on a recruitment programme which made household names of those chosen to bring the nation's sporting events to the listeners tuning in at home. John Arlott became synonymous with cricket, Max Robertson was the public's link to the tennis courts at Wimbledon, whilst Eamonn Andrews and Raymond Glendenning seemed to relish the opportunity of relating every gory detail that took place in the boxing ring.

Into this heady mix of illustrious sports commentators was thrown a young, inexperienced journalist who was to be the voice of sport in Wales and beyond – Alun Williams. Following a gruelling interview by a number of BBC executives who had travelled down to Cardiff from London, the young Williams was congratulated on his successful appointment.

However, before the champagne cork was even popped, the reality of what the job entailed suddenly hit home. Alun Williams's brief was to cover the arts and sport in Wales – no mean feat for a raw, new recruit. To his credit, he rose to all the challenges thrown at him to become the voice of the Corporation in Wales. His clear, concise descriptions of such diverse sports as swimming, athletics, rugby and football, coverage of the Olympic and British Empire and Commonwealth Games, national events and musical extravaganzas was a joy. (Another broadcaster in the same multi-talented mould as Alun was Rex Alston, king of the airwaves for more than twenty years at the end of the Second World War.)

Following his initial euphoria at gaining such a prestigious job, Alun's celebrations were quickly deflated when he was given his first assignment. Glamorgan County Cricket Club were playing Worcestershire at St Helen's on the following Saturday and he was duly appointed to commentate on the game. Keen as he was to make a good impression, he was also extremely nervous and was at pains to point out to his producer that his grasp of cricket was extremely limited. It is true to say that he had played some cricket on the beach at Barry Island and Porthcawl while on the annual Sunday School trips, and had even had some tuition at school so that he knew, at least, the field positions and the laws of the game, but that was the extent of his knowledge. However, his remarks to his enthusiastic producer fell on deaf ears.

The following morning a large brown envelope filled with some useful tips from the producer landed on his doormat, and included the following words of wisdom:

> You may want to say something along the lines of: from the commentary box you'll be able to see the Mumbles Railway and Swansea Bay . . . to your left the Brangwyn Hall and the Patti Pavilion – a godsend to someone like you with a passionate interest in music and the arts . . . and, in front, the rugby ground with all its pageant and history, and in the distance those splendid views towards Mumbles. And then, from time to time, tell us what's happening on the field of play.

Whilst all this was beneficial, it did nothing to pacify the butterflies fluttering madly in the pit of his stomach. For days beforehand he would slip away to the front parlour, concentrate his mind and go over and over (pardon the pun) in his head what he was going to say. He would start by saying: 'This is Alun Williams at St Helen's in Swansea . . . Glamorgan are playing Worcestershire . . . Glamorgan have won the toss and have elected to bat.'

This reminded him of the time when, as a child, he had gone through the same process before taking part in recitation competitions in local eisteddfodau. It had worked then, and there was no reason to suppose that it would not be effective again. 'This is Alun Williams at St Helen's in Swansea . . . Glamorgan are playing Worcestershire . . . and Glamorgan have won the toss and have elected to bat.'

Saturday morning arrived far too soon, and on the journey down the A48 from Cardiff to Swansea, the towns and villages of St Nicholas, Bonvilston, Cowbridge, Pyle, Port Talbot all zoomed past. Again he repeated the words to himself: 'This is Alun Williams at St Helen's in Swansea . . . Glamorgan are playing Worcestershire . . . Glamorgan have won the toss and have elected to bat.'

By the time he arrived at Swansea, he was word perfect. In those days games were three-day contests played from Saturday to Tuesday with a rest day on Sunday. Wickets were pitched at 11.30am with a lunch break from 1.30pm to 2.10pm, and at that very time, when play re-started, the BBC Welsh Home Service was timed to join Alun for live cricket commentary. He had arranged everything neatly in the commentary box – a pile of sandwiches and a couple of bottles of Corona's own Dandelion and Burdock stood to the right of the desk, with the team lists, pen pictures and scorecard perfectly positioned in front of him. The headphones and microphone were plugged in and in good working order. He was ready to go. The red light was on in Cardiff and with ten seconds to broadcast time and with his heart pounding, he heard the continuity presenter state the following words:

> It's now time for cricket and it's over to Alun Williams at St Helen's in Swansea . . . Glamorgan are playing Worcestershire . . . Glamorgan have won the toss and have elected to bat.

It certainly was a tough baptism but Alun proved in no time that he had the confidence, calmness, authority and poise to succeed.

14
The Welsh Connection

What is the common factor that links Alfred Louis Valentine, Gilbert Parkhouse and Jack Mercer? The answer is simple if not obvious – St Helen's. In his 2004 obituary to Valentine, the respected cricket journalist Tony Crozier wrote in *The Independent* that one of the major influences on the West Indies bowler's career was none other than the Glamorgan player, Jack Mercer.

Mercer played for Glamorgan during the 1930s and his record of ten wickets in an innings at the County Ground, New Road, Worcestershire in July 1936 stands to this present day: 26-10-51-10. A medium-paced swing bowler, Mercer's

Jack Mercer, the only Glamorgan bowler to have taken all ten wickets in an innings in a Championship match.

strength was his accuracy – his length and line always immaculate, often deceiving the batsmen in the air and off the seam.

When his first-class career came to an end, Mercer embarked on a successful stint as a coach. Much of this time was spent in the Caribbean, where he came across a young lad devoted to cricket. Not only was the young Valentine passionate about the game but he was also eager to learn and take advice. His main attribute, however, was his self-discipline. When his peers had had enough for the day, Valentine would carry on practising and practising so that he could get the ball to land on the proverbial sixpence.

His persistence and dedication were suitably rewarded when, at the age of nineteen, he was selected as a member of the West Indies team to tour England. Despite his lack of experience at the highest level, the West Indies captain Jack Goddard and vice-captain Jeffrey Stollmeyer had every faith in the new prodigy. This faith was vindicated when Valentine and Sonny Ramadhin played a major part in the first test at Old Trafford. Making his debut, and in conditions which were alien to him, the young bowler took eight wickets (the first five before lunch) in the first innings on a rain-affected pitch. His final analysis proved mightily impressive:

ENGLAND v. WEST INDIES 1950 (1st Test)

L. Hutton	b Valentine	39
R.T. Simpson	c Goddard b Valentine	27
W.J. Edrich	c Gomez b Valentine	7
G.H.G. Doggart	c Rae b Valentine	29
H.E. Dollery	c Gomez b Valentine	8
N.W.D. Yardley	c Gomez b Valentine	0
T.E. Bailey	not out	82
T.G. Evans	c and b Valentine	104
J.C. Laker	b Valentine	0
W.E. Hollies	c Weekes b Ramadhin	0
R. Berry	b Ramadhin	0
Extras	(B8, LB 3, NB 1)	12
Total		312

	O	M	R	W
Valentine	50	14	104	8

This was the first time that the West Indies had won a test match in England and Valentine's bowling figures were testimony to an impressive performance. The jubilation was repeated two months later when the visitors won a second test and, as it turned out, the series when they defeated the old enemy by an innings and 36 runs. Carnival scenes were seen from Kingston to Port-of-Spain, from Bridgetown to Georgetown. Valentine's bowling figures in this second test at Lord's were even more impressive – the young lad from the deprived Spanish Town district of Kingston bowled 116 overs (including 75 maidens) taking 7 wickets for 127 runs.

Included in the England team at Lord's was Gilbert Parkhouse, the Glamorgan opening batsman. A classically stylish batsman, Parkhouse fell victim to Valentine's accuracy, being out for a duck in the first innings and then caught by Goddard for 48, again off Valentine's bowling, in the second innings. Valentine's total of 33 wickets in his first test series (a record which still stands) remains one of the iconic cricketing performances.

Alf Valentine played at St Helen's on two occasions. The first time was in 1957 when he took the wickets of Peter Walker, David Evans and Don Shepherd – the visitors won by 6 wickets. The second visit was in 1963 when Eifion Jones fell victim to the charismatic West Indian bowler, the game ending in a draw.

Master batsman: Gilbert Parkhouse.

15
McConnon's Magic Spell

Much of Alun Howells and Alan Bowen Evans's summer teenage years were spent on a South Wales Transport double decker between Upper Brynaman and St Helen's. And whilst the routine and route might have been the same each time, there were some journeys that were somehow more rewarding than others.

During the 1948 Championship winning season, they had watched in awe as J.C. Clay, Stan Trick and Len Muncer cast their spells. They had marvelled as Emrys Davies, Jim Pleass, Willie Jones and Arthur Dyson excelled with the bat and had appreciated some of the best fielders in the world plying their craft. According to the two Brynamanites, very few could emulate such cricketers as Gilbert Parkhouse, Wilfred Wooller, Willie Jones and the splendid Allan Watkins.

Jim McConnon,
scourge of the South Africans.

During the August Bank Holiday in 1951, that red double-decker bus from Upper Brynaman was bursting at the seams – cricket followers had purchased tickets beforehand for the visit of the South African tourists. They wanted to witness their heroes in the shape of Johnny Waite, Roy Endean, Clive van Ryneveld, Dudley Nourse and Hugh Tayfield. This was a star-spangled XI and were the bookies' firm favourites to defeat Wilfred Wooller's Glamorgan.

Fifty-six years later, Alun and Alan still remember every detail relating to the match and the weekend, including the images glimpsed as the bus travelled to Swansea via Pontardawe, Clydach and Morriston. A co-passenger on that AEC bus that day was Amman Williams, a schoolmaster at Nantgaredig and the brother of Freddie, a charismatic local postman. Amman was looking forward immensely to the match and the occasion, and felt that Glamorgan had a real chance of defeating the Springboks. Overnight rain had drenched the outfield but umpires Parkin and Todd were confident that play would commence promptly at 11.30am, thanks to a stiff breeze blowing in from Swansea Bay. A vociferous crowd of 25,000 were not to be disappointed. The South African captain, Dudley Nourse, won the toss and invited Glamorgan to bat first, and that decision was vindicated thanks to the efforts of bowlers Mansell and Rowan. They took advantage of the overcast conditions and Wooller's men were back in the pavilion by mid-afternoon, having being bowled out for 111 – a total which was not nearly enough according to many knowledgeable Glamorgan supporters.

However, the experienced Glamorgan skipper, Wilfred Wooller was still up-beat and confident. He knew that batting would be difficult for the visitors; the ball was deviating in all directions and, at tea, South Africa were 36-7 with Wooller and Muncer proving virtually unplayable. Mansell and Rowan came to the rescue with a battling stand of 52 and, at close of play on the Saturday, the visitors were dismissed for 111 with Rowan bringing the innings to a close with two gigantic sixes. The experts were lost for words – twenty wickets in a day! Was it the early morning rain which was responsible? Some even consulted the tide tables but came to no firm conclusions. The large crowd had been royally entertained, Wooller (3-41) and Muncer (7-45) being congratulated at the end of a great day's cricket.

The excitement was infectious on the return journey to Brynaman – the general consensus was that the day's play had been stimulating and there were many opinions and views expressed on how Glamorgan should approach their second innings. Everyone agreed that a total in excess of 200 was paramount and it was with a great deal of anticipation that Amman Williams and the two young schoolboys looked forward to Monday morning.

Both sides agreed to keep the covers on the wicket over the weekend and, when the players arrived for early morning practice, the moisture had disappeared and the cricket square was as dry as the Sahara. The spinners, Rowan (South Africa) and McConnon (Glamorgan) gleefully rubbed their hands, realising that there was a real chance of a bumper crop. Batting proved difficult for the determined Glamorgan batsmen; Mansell and Rowan shared the spoils and the only two to make any headway were Jim Pleass (29) and skipper Wooller with a dashing 46. The supporters who had returned en masse were in total agreement – South Africa to win with ease.

Waite and Endean were in authoritative mood – they only required 148 for victory and when they added 54 for the first wicket, Amman Williams decided it was time to head for downtown Swansea and an early bus back to Brynaman. Other supporters trickled from the ground; a win for the tourists was surely inevitable but the two Amman Valley youngsters remained – they had been told at school and on the local cricket ground, 'It's not over until the final ball has been bowled.' Amman reached home in good time and, in an age prior to hourly bulletins on radio and 24-hour television coverage, announced to a waiting throng that South Africa had won by a country mile.

The temperature was rising back at St Helen's. Muncer and McConnon both claimed a wicket apiece; Wooller brilliantly caught van Ryneveld within a hair's breadth of the bat. Within a few overs, South Africa slumped to 61-4 when Muncer deceived Cheetham, and the athletic Watkins held on to the catch. The crowd were ecstatic, they were at fever pitch as mission impossible slowly became plausible. 'I was seated near the steps,' recalled Alun, and honestly couldn't believe what was happening. The visitors were in a mounting state of panic – most of the team had already changed and were ready to celebrate before returning to London via High Street Station. And then, came that over, which changed the state and course of the match.'

McConnon was the bowler. Cheetham was caught with ease by Allan Watkins, his third catch of the innings, before Clift held on to a difficult chance off Melle. The tension was unbearable and when McConnon clean bowled Fullerton on the hat-trick ball, the ground just erupted – this was truly sensational cricket. I wonder whether Amman Williams heard the din in Upper Brynaman? From being 54-0, the Springboks were now 68-7. A hat-trick to Jim McConnon – the fourth Glamorgan player to achieve the feat following in the footsteps of Tom Arnott, Jack Mercer and Emrys Davies, but the very first at St Helen's. The atmosphere was quite electric, but, as the bowlers started on their run, an eerie silence descended on the playing arena. Gilbert Parkhouse patrolled the boundary as 12th man and within minutes the aggressive Rowan lofted a Muncer delivery skywards in his direction. Parkhouse held on to the catch to secure a quite astonishing victory. McConnon was the hero; he took 6-27 and Dudley Nourse's men readily accepted that they had been deceived by a bowler who was virtually unplayable on the day.

The supporters streamed on to the field of play to acknowledge their heroes. It required a superhuman effort to get to the pavilion; the National Anthem was sung with gusto, the champagne flowed to recognise a truly magnificent victory. Alun and Alan saw every ball bowled, and even on a glorious autumnal day in 2007, still romanticised about the events surrounding the victory. Amman Williams, 'Read all about it in Tuesday morning's *Western Mail*!'

16

St Helen's and Rugby League

by Robert Gate

In rugby-league land, the St Helen's ground means Knowsley Road and 'has nowt to do wi Swansea'. However, life was not always thus. The St Helen's Ground, Swansea, was for a brief time after the war the home ground of the Wales Rugby League international side, a situation not much to the liking of the Welsh Rugby Union. Thankfully, it was beyond their control because the ground was then municipally owned and the Rugby Football League was able to hire it from Swansea Council. Eleven rugby league internationals were staged there during that period and a further four in the 1970s. The games, with attendances, were:

ST. HELEN'S GROUND, SWANSEA
SATURDAY, NOV. 20th, 1943
KICK-OFF — 3.15 P.M.

GREAT SERVICES
RUGBY INTERNATIONAL
WALES
v.
ENGLAND

IN AID OF
THE NAVY - THE ARMY
AND R.A.F. CHARITIES

Official Programme: 3d.

Nov 24, 1945	Wales 11	England 3	30,000
Nov 16, 1946	Wales 5	England 19	25,000
April 12, 1947	Wales 17	France 15	20,000
Oct 18, 1947	Wales 20	New Zealand 28	18,283
Dec 6, 1947	Wales 7	England 18	10,000
March 20, 1948	Wales 12	France 20	6,500
Oct 23, 1948	Wales 9	France 12	12,032
Nov 20,1948	Wales 5	Australia 12	9,224
Feb 5, 1949	Wales 14	England 10	9,553
Nov 12, 1949	Wales 16	France 8	4,749
March 31, 1951	Wales 21	Other Nationalities 27	5,000
Feb16, 1975	Wales 21	France 8	15,000
Oct 19, 1975	Wales 6	Australia 18	11,112*
Nov 2, 1975	Wales 25	New Zealand 24	2,645*
Oct 15, 1978	Wales 3	Australia 8	4,250

*World Championship fixtures

Although Wales were not particularly successful when playing at St Helen's, the ground does still hold the record attendance for a Wales RL home game, which was the 30,000 for the 11-3 victory over England in 1945. That game was the first rugby-league international to be staged after the Second

World War ended – indeed, it was the first international fixture of either code in the post-war period. Wales, captained by the immortal Gus Risman (Salford), earned £7 a man for their victory but would no doubt have played for nothing, particularly those who were old All Whites, such as stand-off W.T.H. Davies (Bradford Northern) and second rower Doug Phillips (Oldham). Risman kicked the only goal of the game and Wales's try scorers were Gareth Price (Leeds, formerly Llanelli), who claimed two, and loose forward Ike Owens (Leeds, formerly Maesteg).

Gareth Price, a brainy, hard-tackling centre, had a couple of unusual experiences at St Helen's. In the game against New Zealand in 1947, he laid out the referee, Stan Adams from Hull, who foolishly got in his way as he burst through the Kiwi ranks. Six months earlier, Price had been selected to captain Wales against France at St Helen's. Price lived in Swansea at the time and a dispute arose as to whether he should stay at the team's official HQ at a local hotel. The upshot was that he did not and consequently lost the captaincy to Doug Phillips. Price never did get to skipper Wales.

Wigan's Ted Ward was one centre who did get to captain Wales, leading them in six of those internationals at St Helen's. Ward, another former Llanelli player, kicked three goals in the defeat against France in March 1948 but was dead on his feet by the last quarter. He had been up all the previous night with neuralgia and had to have teeth extracted at 5.30am! Wales's problems were compounded by Monsieur Pascal from Toulouse, the first Frenchman to referee rugby league in Wales. His penalty count was 18-1 against the Welshmen and he had a weird and wonderful interpretation of how the ball should be played. According to the *Sunday Dispatch*, he 'constantly had the crowd in uproar'.

Ward, an extremely talented centre three-quarter, had joined Wigan Rugby League Club in 1937. Just after the Second World War, he had been selected to represent the Great Britain team (captained by Gus Risman) to tour Australia in 1946. His performances resulted in rave reviews in the Australian newspapers with many teams determined to sign him. It would have been financially beneficial for the young Ward but he was unsure and sought advice. He immediately sent a telegram back to his mother in Garnant outlying the nature of the contract. Within hours, the Australian Post Office delivered a message to the team hotel, a message which just had the four words – 'Ted, come home. Mam.'

Unquestionably, the finest of the St Helen's internationals was the last of the immediate post-war period when Wales lost 21-27 to the celebrated Other Nationalities XIII in 1951. A coruscating game produced 12 tries, but only five for Wales. Swansea rugby enthusiasts would never again have the opportunity to see icons of rugby league, such as Brian Bevan, Lionel Cooper, Arthur Clues and Dave Valentine.

Swansea people did, however, have earlier chances to see many of rugby league's greatest figures in the myriad of Services games played at St Helen's in the period 1942-45. Trevor Foster and Idwal Davies spoke for many rugby league and rugby union men when they told me that wartime rugby was the most enjoyable they had experienced. Trevor, ex-Pill Harriers and Newport, joined Bradford Northern in 1938 and was still with the club, by then Bradford Bulls, as its time-keeper, when he died aged 90 on April 2, 2005. Although the war cut a swathe through his career, he always maintained that it enhanced it by allowing him to play at the highest levels of both codes, with and against their greatest players. Among the men he most admired were Swansea's legendary halfbacks Haydn Tanner, whom Trevor described as the 'nearest thing to Gareth Edwards', and Willie (W.T.H.) Davies, the merlinesque stand-off with whom he shared so many triumphs at Bradford.

Services international at St Helen's. W.T.H. Davies is introduced to local dignitaries.

Trevor was arguably the finest forward in both codes during the war – second-row in league and wing-forward in union. Swansea became a home from home for him as he appeared in many of the big games which St Helen's hosted in aid of Services charities. He figured in all four of the Services internationals Wales played against England at Swansea, all victories, and in games for the Army against South Wales. Interestingly, England met Wales, alternately at Swansea and Gloucester, in eight Services internationals, fully accepting that the Welsh teams were crammed with rugby league men. England also played Scotland regularly. Scotland refused to play Wales simply because they fielded rugby league players, who might contaminate their own players more than the Nazis. It never occurred to them that England often fielded up to half a dozen leaguites who were just as contagious as the Welsh renegades!

SEMI-INTERNATIONAL RUGBY FOOTBALL MATCH IN AID OF BRITISH ARMY CHARITIES AND MAYOR OF SWANSEA'S WAR COMFORTS FUND

The BRITISH ARMY
v.
SOUTH WALES
ST. HELEN'S GROUND, SWANSEA
SATURDAY, DEC. 20, 1941
KICK-OFF 3 P.M.

OFFICIAL SOUVENIR
PROGRAMME - - 3d.
Total proceeds in aid of above Funds.

57

17
Tiger Bay, Wigan and St Helen's

It was a gesture to warm the heart and proved that honesty, sincerity and respect have the upper hand on selfishness and apathy. To us in Wales (and to those knowledgeable supporters of Wigan), the climax of the 2003/04 rugby season was reached on a sweltering afternoon at the Millennium Stadium, Cardiff on May 15. Two North of England teams, Wigan and St Helen's, travelled to the Welsh capital to contest the final of the Powergen Challenge Cup, one of rugby league's premier occasions. The Saints were victorious, but from a personal and national perspective, it wasn't the on-field exploits that stood out, but rather one significant event that occurred before the kick-off.

It is customary for the teams in the final to be led on to the field by fat-cat presidents in Armani suits or suitably important and preoccupied managers. 2004 was different. A fortnight or so before the game, senior officials at Wigan had announced that it would be a native of Tiger Bay that would precede the team on its procession from the security of the changing room to the field of battle. The citizens of the industrial town in Lancashire had decided to immortalize one of the Britain's greatest sporting greats, the genial giant, Billy Boston.

Wales's hold on Billy Boston may well have been a tenuous one; by 1953, he had bid farewell to the land of his birth and settled in Wigan, and it was this town, and the North-west of England, that would be his home and heartland subsequently. Since Boston was of mixed-race background, it may well be that Wigan's long-established reputation for attracting players from all corners of the globe had persuaded him to head north. Many believe that Boston had encountered racial prejudice in his relationship (or lack of one) with rugby union. Others claimed that he had failed to see the doors of opportunity opening for him in the fifteen-a-side game.

Aneirin Rhys Thomas crystallizes Billy Boston perfectly in *Cewri Campau Cymru*:

> All are agreed on his proverbial abilities, and all describe him as the complete player. Boston lit up the town of Wigan with his brilliant skills. Wigan was a bleak industrial town in the 1950s. A town of coal mines and austere factories, a town that bore the scars of the Second World War all too clearly. Escaping the yellow fog on a cold winter Saturday to watch the sparkling genius of Billy Boston at Central Park lit up the soul and warmed the body. Here, he was king.

A player who combined the speed of Martin Offiah, the guile and magic of Gerald Davies and the power of John Bevan is a mouth-watering prospect. One

One of Wales's truly great rugby players, Billy Boston, about to join his captain on the pitch.

such was Billy Boston. And in Cardiff on that May afternoon, he was the object of the dignified respect of the common man and woman; the common men and women of Wigan and the North of England!

Aneirin Rhys Thomas continues:

> He was an amiable king, a king of the people. Maybe Wigan's back-to-back terraced houses, Wigan's smoke chimneys, the pub-and-club Wigan, the rugby-talking Wigan was akin to Tiger Bay when Boston was back in Wales.

There were similarities in background and geography maybe, but Saturday, May 15, 2004 proved that the citizens of Wigan were warmer, fairer, cleverer and wiser than us Welshmen.

Undoubtedly, if a role model for a better future is required, Billy Boston's your man. St Helen's has witnessed many memorable rugby-league contests, the majority of which were international matches, but none were played unfortunately during the great winger's era.

Billy Boston's connection with the Mumbles Road arena dates from his childhood when he played for Cardiff Secondary Schools (under 15) against Swansea. And the proof? Well, thanks to Mike Nicholas, I was given the phone number of that notoriously ferocious forward, Jim Mills, and the conversation proved an entertaining one:

Alun Bevan: Mr. Mills . . . we've never met before but I wonder whether you could help me. I'm trying to find out whether Billy Boston played at St Helen's in Swansea.

Jim Mills: I suppose you know I played a few matches on the ground! I'll tell you what I'll do. I live in Wigan so I'll pop down to see him during the morning and ring you back later on. How's that?

Some three hours later, Jim Mills called to say that Billy Boston had confirmed that he had indeed played for the blue-and-blacks on the historic ground. I couldn't help grinning, delighted that another of the greats had graced this ground.

18
Gilbert Parkhouse

It was over a coffee and some toasted teacakes at Verdi's in Mumbles that I casually asked the great Don Shepherd about the qualities which made Gilbert Parkhouse such an outstanding opening batsmen. Almost immediately, Don was in full flow – I turned on the mini-disk player, sat back and listened. Praise from a playing colleague is praise indeed! This is what he had to say:

Stylish opening batsman, Gilbert Parkhouse, who thrilled the St Helen's faithful in the 1950s and 1960s.

The very mention of Gilbert Parkhouse will, for many, evoke memories of an elegant right-handed batsman who opened for Glamorgan with great distinction for many seasons and always appeared to be fully at ease against the quickest and most hostile of fast bowlers in the world. There were many of true quality: Statham, Loader, Trueman, and Tyson; Lindwall and Miller; Heine and Adcock; Hall and Griffith and many more. All were instantly judged on line and length, and played accordingly, from either front or back foot, with perfect technique and wonderful timing.

Frequently, one wondered how one so slim could propel the ball through the covers at such a velocity. Gilbert was never intimidated by short-pitched deliveries and, more often than not, would accept the implied challenge by hooking or pulling with power. And this was before the age of protective helmets!

Faced by the certainty of having to play many matches on wet, slow or turning pitches, he honed his skills to deal with many class spinners plying their cunning trade. Gilbert was one of the very few to read the variations of the great Sonny Ramadhin. The sweep shot and the delicate late-cut became major sources of runs, and by the mid 1950s he was the complete batsman and regularly topped the Glamorgan run aggregate. But for great contemporary opening batsmen – Len Hutton, Cyril Washbrook, Reg Simpson and others of high class – Parky would have gained more than seven caps and one major tour to Australia. Most games came effortlessly to him. He was a fine rugby player for the All Whites, he played hockey for Wales and badminton to a high standard but he excelled at cricket, as one would expect of a lad born within a six-hit of St Helen's and coached in his formative years by the legendary W.J. Bancroft of Swansea, Glamorgan and Wales fame. Gilbert is, without doubt, one of the all-time Glamorgan greats and it was always a pleasure to play alongside him and watch him at the crease.

19
W.O. Williams

W.O. Williams (Swansea, Wales and British Lions) – powerful loose-head prop forward.

Like the special ingredient handed down in an old family recipe, or the combination to the vault at Fort Knox, what goes on in the front row of a scrum is a secret known only to a select few. It is an apprenticeship: its specialized knowledge is passed on through word of mouth and the education of actions, and there aren't many who can be considered masters of the craft.

Those who have tasted the experience of playing in the front row of the scrum compare it with a period spent in a medieval dungeon, or a shift in the cramped conditions on the coal face. It is certainly not for the faint-hearted. It is true that modern players need to be athletic and the hours which they spend in the gymnasium have completely altered the physical demeanour of the front-row forward. They are now seen to be running all over the field, tackling anyone that moves, and even at times forming part of the back line in support of a wing three-quarter! Some wonder, however, that all this been at the expense of perfecting their own peculiar stock-in-trade?

The prop forward is traditionally seen as a man mountain; a strong, physical, solid individual with a powerful upper body. His primary function is to maintain stability in the scrummage. Over the years, Swansea has produced many prop forwards who have gone on to win international honours, including William Joseph, the Rev. Alban Davies, Tom Parker, David Jenkins, Tom Day, Harry Payne, Eddie Morgan, Dai Jones, W.O. Williams, Phil Llewellyn, Clive Williams, David Young, Stuart Evans, Christian Loader, Ian Buckett, Chris Anthony, Darren Morris and Ben Evans.

William Owen Williams, or Billy Williams, who hailed from Gowerton, won 22 caps for his country and four test caps for the British Lions during their successful tour of South Africa in 1955. W.O. started his playing career as a mobile and abrasive second-row forward before 'The Big Five', in their wisdom, chose him at loose-head prop forward for Wales against France at Stade Colombes in 1951. This was an amazing selectorial decision – this was his very first appearance in the front row at any level and the press were scathing in their criticism. John Christopher, the *South Wales Evening Post*'s reporter, was also taken aback, 'Why choose W.O. at prop forward? There are far better front-row forwards in Wales.' Wales lost the match 8-3, but W.O. held his own and vindicated the selectors' confidence in his ability.

At St Helen's, the selectors refused to be swayed by national pressure and W.O. remained in the second row for the visit of the South Africans on December 15, 1951 – the All Whites performed heroically but eventually lost a titanic battle by 11-3. Dil Johnson crossed for an early try but 'Chum' Ochse replied with a similar score with 'Okey' Geffin converting and adding a late penalty goal. A week later and W.O. was selected at loose-head prop for his country against Muller's Springboks, a match Wales should have won convincingly. In his third game for Wales, Cliff Morgan kicked too often and too waywardly with the ball consistently landing in the secure hands of fullback Johnny Buchler. With Roy John magnificent in the line-out and the Welsh forwards outplaying their opponents, it was disappointing to see so much clean possession wasted. An Ochse try and Brewis dropped goal gave the visitors a 6-0 lead before Wales replied in spectacular fashion in the dying minutes. Gwilliam fed back from the line-out with an underarm pass to Cliff Morgan. Bleddyn Williams and Malcolm Thomas worked a scissors and Bleddyn strode through for the try. Too little too late – South Africa won 6-3. Remarkably, Wales's tight-head prop forward in this match was none other than Don Hayward from Newbridge, who had also been converted from the second row!

W.O.'s future was now secure and Swansea soon realised that the Gowerton boilermaker would be a major asset in the All Whites boiler-room. Williams was by now a keen student of the mechanics of scrummaging – he was determined to perfect the art. His smile might have been warm and mischievous, but there was a compulsion to strain nerve and sinew.

He took his responsibilities in the scrum very seriously, and his aim at all times was to make sure that his hooker was well served. To this end he employed a whole range of techniques, which varied according to which scrum half was to feed the ball into the scrum. If it was a Swansea put in, then W.O. had his feet planted solidly on the ground and used his considerable strength and know-how to maintain equilibrium and provide a clear path for the hooker to get to the ball.

The commanding presence of W.O. Williams.

On the other hand, if the opposing side had the put-in, then different strategies were employed, not of all of them adhering strictly to the law book! W.O. relished this role, that of causing chaos in a defensive scrum. His aim, of course, was to bring down his opponent so that their hooker was unsighted, and all without attracting the attention of the referee. He was so adept at this that the movement often went undetected until the damage had been done.

On December 12, 1953, W.O. Williams played an absolute blinder in a 6-6 draw with the mighty All Blacks at St Helen's. John Faull, Swansea's reserve centre and playing in only his third match for the club, kicked two monstrous penalty goals which eventually cancelled out two Elsom tries. Jim Rees, Dil Johnson, Len Blyth and Clem Thomas also deserve special mention along with the entire team who rose magnificently to the occasion. Seven days later and W.O. (along with Clem Thomas) were included in the Welsh team to face R.C. Stuart's All Blacks, a match which will go down in the annals of Welsh rugby history as one of our finest ever performances. The score was 8-8 with five minutes remaining when Clem Thomas dashed down the left-hand touchline and cross-kicked for Ken Jones to collect with ease before racing behind the posts. The All Blacks had yet to beat Wales at the Arms Park!

If 1953 had been memorable, then 1955 proved just as significant. The Swansea front-row forward was selected to represent the British Lions in South Africa and played in all four tests against the rampant Springboks. W.O. packed down with Courtenay Meredith and Bryn Meredith providing a Welsh foundation for several impressive performances. They tied the series 2-2 and W.O. Williams was rewarded for his gutsy displays with the vice-captaincy for the third test match at Pretoria, a match the Lions won by 9-6.

In these times of ever-evolving technology, there is still a need for certain practical skills. These may include plumbing, carpentry, roofing, and most certainly front-row know-how. W.O. Williams was certainly a master in this art.

20
One Cap Wonder

Bryan Richards, the All Whites outside half, set pulses racing at St Helen's and throughout England and Wales during the 1950s and early 1960s. He had that touch of magic, that wizardry and uncanny judgement which prompts rugby followers to leap out of their seats in sheer disbelief. His defence-splitting runs excited even opposition supporters; he was as unpredictable as a firework and possessed that spark of genius which made him a true match-winner.

However, for some unknown reason, he seemed surplus to requirements at international level. The Welsh 'Big Five' consistently ignored the qualities exhibited by the exciting Richards. Why? The fly half possessed the flair and guile to unlock defences – he was the Gerald Davies and Mark Ring of his generation.

The selectors, who desperately wanted to revolutionise Welsh rugby and recreate the good old days of the early 1950s, when Wales won two Grand Slams, seemed unimpressed by Richards's gifts and talents. I suppose they thought he was too small, not strong enough for the rigours of international rugby.

Peter Thompson, the great Australian golfer once said, 'Coaching has become big business. I count myself lucky that I received no coaching.' Bryan Richards was a natural, in the mould of other St Helen's greats and deserved to be recognised at the highest level. His one cap against France at Cardiff in 1960 (no ball and no opportunity) was scant reward for a player who displayed such killer instinct and innate ability. The French became world leaders in the game without losing their raison d'être and it's true to say that the flair, the panache, the ability to counter-attack is still plain for all to see. Bryan Richards would have won fifty caps for the *Tricolores* but was sadly kicked into touch in Wales – am I missing something? Anyone for *bando* or yoga!

21
Swansea's American Royalty

St Helen's has been nothing if not accommodating. It has hosted an array of sports, including one that is more all-American than All White.

In the 1960s, the council were obliged to cover part of the old field with a succession of wooden boards in preparation for a particularly bizarre visit, that of those athletes-cum-entertainers extraordinaire, the Harlem Globetrotters. The New York-based basketball team drew thousands to their venues, playing exhibition rather than competitive games. They included in their ranks the 'Clown Prince' himself, Meadowlark Lemon, who played in more than 7,500 consecutive games for the red, white, and blue. He played before Popes, Kings, Queens and Presidents in more than 94 countries around the world, in more than 1,500 North American cities and . . . at St Helen's in Swansea.

22
A Wizard on the Wing

In my book, first impressions count. It was 1999 and we were travelling along the winding road that takes you from Mendoza in Argentina to Santiago in Chile. All around us, nature was at her best, the autumnal colours of the trees vying for attention with the splendour of the Andes and the deep valleys below. Then, all of a sudden, into view came the breathtaking sight of Cerra Aconcagua, the continent's highest peak. We first had to stop the car, take in the scene and record it all on camera. The geography of the region had been a part of our 'A' level studies but nothing could have prepared me for this moment.

Man-made creations can also have this effect on an individual – consider the Guggenheim Museum in Bilbao as an example. One can walk around Frank Gehry's incredible creation all day and appreciate differing angles and contours. 'How wiggly can you get and still make a building?' was the question posed by the Canadian architect? He was daring enough to put his theories to the test and, in so doing, produced a masterpiece.

The same sense of daring when carried over into the sporting arena can produce the most unlikely result. Lillian Board was the favourite to win the 400-metres Olympic title in Mexico City in 1968, the Essex athlete having swept the 'board' in all major events leading up to the games and the result was considered a foregone conclusion. But no one had told Colette Besson. Board led the field to the last metre but then Besson appeared from nowhere, overtook her dramatically and won the gold medal. What a way to make a first impression!

Dewi Bebb's arrival on the St Helen's rugby field did not go unnoticed either. The *South Wales Evening Post* reporter Ron Griffiths often used the word 'wizard' to describe the lightning-fast winger from North Wales who shone whilst playing for the All Whites, Wales and the Lions during the late 1950s and 1960s. Having spent two years in the Navy, Bebb decided to take a teacher-training course in Trinity College, Carmarthen, and within a short space of time he was making his mark on the left wing for Swansea. His first appearance in the white shirt was a baptism of fire – the 'Jacks' facing the 'Turks' at Stradey Park. The twenty-year-old's incredible try at the beginning of the second half achieved the impossible: praise from both the Swansea and Llanelli supporters. 'Bebb . . . has brains and pace – much more is going to be heard of him', wrote 'Scarlet' in the *Evening Post*. A number of players have the opportunity to play at the highest level but fail to shine. Other players, due to their natural ability, positive attitude and dose of good luck manage to show their true colours and this was Dewi Bebb's story. Ron Griffiths campaigned for Bebb to don the red shirt during his first season with Swansea, but overall the public response was that Ron was getting carried away and that Bebb needed to perfect his game before entering the international stage.

No finer sight at St Helen's: Dewi Bebb in full flight.

The 'Big Five' took heed of the chief rugby reporter's message and on January 17, 1959, less than six weeks since he'd worn the Swansea rugby shirt for the first time, the young man from Bangor was facing the old enemy, England, at Cardiff Arms Park. Having played a mere five games for the All Whites, Dewi was one of seven players to receive their first Welsh caps in that particular game against England. The other six were Malcolm Price, Haydn Davies, Cliff Ashton, Derek Main, Ian Ford and John Leleu.

In atrocious conditions and with the pitch resembling a lake, the Welsh forwards, under the leadership of Clem Thomas, bulldozed their way around the field. It was not long before their efforts produced, what turned out to be, the only try of the match but it was a decisive score. Howard Evans takes up the story in his book *Welsh International Matches 1881-2000*:

> Dewi Bebb marked his debut with a try typical of the opportunism he always displayed. After 30 minutes of play he threw into a lineout, took the return from second-row forward R.H. Williams and swerved past Peter Jackson and Jim Hetherington to score for Terry Davies to convert with a fine kick. Spectators carried the Swansea wing three-quarter off shoulder-high at the end of the match.

David Smith and Gareth Williams in *Fields of Praise state*: 'As dusk descended . . . the rain still falling relentlessly, and Wales mounting a squelching forward assault in defence of that five-point lead, the crowd packed under the North Stand and sensing the danger was over, broke into an emotional, hair-prickling rendering of *Hen Wlad fy Nhadau*. Spontaneously, harmoniously, perfectly pitched, unpunctuated by cheering or applause, the majestic anthem rolled across the ground, enveloping and sustaining its exhausted heroes in an unforgettable expression of relief and gratitude.'

To complete the historical significance of this scene, standing on the rain-soaked terraces watching his first international was none other than Gareth Edwards. He had travelled to Cardiff with Huw Llywelyn Davies and Huw's father, Eic, in the latter's grey Rover 75. While Eic sat in the relative comfort of the press box, the two youngsters watched proceedings from near the touchline. They may have got drenched but at the end of the match felt more than a little smug as they were standing right next to the spot where Dewi Bebb scored his try. Ironically, some eight years later, history was to repeat itself, as it was in the exact same spot that Bebb scored his last try for Wales – again against England. And who was there to deliver the scoring pass? None other than the aforementioned Gareth Edwards!

So what was the secret of Dewi Bebb's success as a rugby player? What exactly were the qualities of the winger who donned the Welsh shirt 34 times between 1959 and 1967? His speed on the rugby field was legendary and I have no doubt that he would have excelled in athletics had he pursued a career in this field. He was also aware of that mathematical principle, 'The shortest distance between two points is a straight line'. Dewi Bebb knew his way to the try-line and whenever the opportunity presented itself, he would rarely miss. Sad to say but the type of rugby played in the Five Nations Championship in the 1960s was not conducive to flamboyant displays by the backs. The forwards lacked power and strength and this inevitably led to a dull, uninspiring pattern of play. Dewi Bebb was one of those who suffered as a result. It was not unusual for the wings to leave the field at the end of the match without having received one pass, as teams defended constantly and relied on a kicking game to get them out of trouble.

Today, there are always tiresome lists of 'the greatest players ever' in our national newspapers. Readers are constantly asked to scrutinize these lists and vote for their sporting heroes. Any discussion of the best wingers past and present inevitably leads to the names of Ken Jones, Gerald Davies, Maurice Richards, John Bevan, J.J. Williams, Ieuan Evans and Shane Williams being mentioned. While no one would dispute those names, I rest assured that had Willie Llewellyn, Reggie Gibbs, J.C. Morley, Geoffrey Rees-Jones and Dewi Bebb been playing in the 1970s, or even today, then the man from Bangor would be a strong contender to be included.

Dewi toured with the British Lions on two occasions. The first time was to South Africa in 1962 and the second to Australia and New Zealand in 1966 when he scored a try against the former in Brisbane. During his career, he scored a total of eleven tries for Wales – six of these against England, a statistic his father W. Ambrose Bebb, who was a staunch Plaid Cymru supporter, would have relished. When his rugby-playing days were over, Dewi became a highly respected television producer, working first for TWW and then HTV at Cardiff. A knowledgeable and conscientious individual, he was down-to-earth, popular and held in high regard by all who knew him – a gentleman who never had a bad word to say about anyone.

The last word goes to the ex-Chairman of Leeds Rugby League Football Club. It was the early 1990s and, due to our work commitments, Dewi and I had travelled to Headingley for the semi-final of the Challenge Cup. The influential administrator and Dewi reminisced about the bygone age, a time when Dewi came close to signing for Leeds having returned from the 1962 Lions tour. When Dewi was out of earshot, the Leeds man confided in me: 'I wanted him to join us because he was a fast, cunning and balanced player. In the thirteen-a-side game character, attitude and flair are vital. Dewi Bebb ticked all the boxes – he would have been legendary.'

23
Top Cat

If Clive Rowlands had been a cricketer, then he would have been the only Welshman ever to have batted, bowled and kept wicket at test level. As a rugby personality, he has done it all. As a player, he captained his country when they won the Triple Crown in season 1964/65; he coached a rampant national team when they won the Grand Slam during season 1970/71; became a national selector for many years before managing the successful British Lions squad, under Finlay Calder's captaincy, to Australia in 1989. Latterly, he has been a part of the commentary team on BBC Radio Cymru where his knowledgeable and witty comments have endeared him to a new generation of rugby followers. Not bad for a youngster from the Swansea valley mining village of Upper Cwmtwrch (and Clive is keen to point out the importance of the 'Upper').

One who has first-hand experience of Clive's dry sense of humour is the other legend from the Swansea valley (also claimed by the Amman valley), Gareth Edwards. During the 1970s when Gareth was playing and Clive was national coach and team selector, the phone lines between Gwauncaegurwen and Upper Cwmtwrch would be red hot and Gareth, as any expectant international, would be keen to find out if he had been included in the Wales team. As Gareth tells it, the conversation went as follows – except that it was originally in Welsh:

Gareth: Margaret . . . can I have a quick word with Clive, please?
Margaret: Clive. Gareth wants a word. Now, Clive!
Clive: Yes, What do you want?
Gareth: Well, the squad is being announced tonight. Am I in the team?
Clive: Gareth . . . I can't tell you! My role as a coach depends on honesty and maintaining a strict code of silence. I know the answer to your question but my lips are sealed.
Gareth: But Clive!
Clive: Sorry, Gareth. We've known each other for quite some time, we're both Welsh speakers and from the same area . . . but I'm unable to say anything.
Gareth: But Clive!
Clive: Look, Gareth. I can't say whether you're in the team. But I can say this – you're not out of the team!!!
Gareth: Thanks, Clive. Have a good night.

And that was the normal state of affairs for nearly twelve years – Gareth aware of his presence in the team before the *Western Mail, Argus, Echo, South Wales Evening Post, BBC* and *TWW*.

Vene, vidi, vici – the motto of the Roman Emperor Julius Caesar and one which Brian Lochore's New Zealand side could easily have adopted following their conquest of Canada, Scotland, England, Wales and France in 1967. In a series of 17 matches, the All Blacks won 16 and drew one (this against an East Wales XV captained by Gareth Edwards). The visitors scored 37 tries while the opposition managed only 8 – two claimed by Welshmen: Hywel Williams for West Wales at St Helen's and Frank Wilson for East Wales at the Arms Park.

For the West Wales encounter with the mighty All Blacks, players were chosen from Aberavon, Neath, Swansea, Llanelli and Maesteg, with Clive a popular and obvious choice as captain. In a pre-match interview, the former international was confident his side could rise to the occasion and defeat what was being described in the press as one of the finest New Zealand sides to visit the Northern Hemisphere. When match day dawned, expectations in and around the Swansea area were high – history was on their side as Swansea, Cardiff and Newport had already beaten the All Blacks in previous encounters (Llanelli would also join the list in 1972).

Wednesday, November 8, 1967 was a bright, sunny day at St Helen's and some 40,000 or more spectators descended on the ground to support the home side. While both teams were deprived of many of their star players (these having been rested in preparation for the international match which would follow three days later), Colin Meads, Kel Tremain and Ken Gray played in both games.

The game developed into a classic encounter with no quarter asked or given on either side. The combined Welsh team were steadfast in their defence and, at the same time, caused a few headaches for their opponents. With half-time approaching, the score stood at 6-0 for the home side, the points coming from two well-struck penalties from the boot of fullback Doug Rees. It was inevitable that New Zealand would retaliate, and this they did in fine fashion with a superbly worked move which resulted in centre three-quarter Graham Thorne sprinting threequarters of the length of the field to score a try underneath the posts. A second try claimed by Colin Meads gave the visitors a 10-6 lead at the interval.

When play resumed, Rees and Kember exchanged penalties and then Clive, who was a source of inspiration, decided to take matters into his own hands. Breaking menacingly from a scrum, he targeted a kick towards the far touchline where wing three-quarter Hywel Williams gave chase. Unfortunately it was All Black fullback Gerald Kember who got to the ball first, but he was promptly floored by Cyril Jones. As the ball spilled from Kember's grasp, Williams was on hand to scoop it up and claim the try.

The crowd went wild with excitement with an array of headgear tossed in the air in jubilation. West Wales were ahead and could have scored on at least two occasions were it not for the questionable decisions of the Bristol referee, Mike Titcomb. Clive was a revelation – his plotting, cunning and leadership skills would have impressed Churchill and Montgomery, and it was his quick thinking and accurate kicking in the direction of his wing three-quarters which caused mayhem in the All Blacks' defence. Again, tries were there for the taking, but Mr Titcomb adjudged Hywel Williams, the New Quay express, to be offside by a matter of a few inches. It was a cruel decision and Clive was furious.

This was a turning point in the match and the visitors went on to score two late tries through Thorne and Going. The final score of 21-14, as is often the case, did not reflect the way the beaten side had played, and Clive, as captain, and coach Carwyn James were quick to praise the superhumam effort of all concerned in putting up such a fine performance.

Clive Rowlands in action for Group Captain Ranji Walker's XV against Swansea at St Helen's.

Clive Rowlands's new sports shop in Morriston. The crafty scrum half celebrates with Gareth Edwards, John Taylor, Mervyn Davies and actor Hywel Bennett.

West Wales: D. Rees, H. Rees, J. Davies, C. Jones, H. Wiliams, K. Evans, C. Rowlands, B. Gale, R. Thomas, W. Williams, B. Davies, D. Thomas, D. Morris, M. Evans, R. Wanbon

New Zealand: Kember, Clarke, Thorne, Steel, Cottrell, Herewini, Going, Gray, Major, Hopkinson, Jennings, Meads, Wills, Tremain, Kirkpatrick

Dennis Busher of the *Daily Express* was most complimentary the following morning: 'For Clive Rowlands, this moment of defeat will be remembered with as much admiration as his list of successes. He threw every trick in the books at the All Blacks, had them rocking on their heels, and was then robbed by sheer misfortune. He showed a full range of repertoire of kicks ranging from the high skyscraper to the carefully calculated chip for his wing to run on to.' Hear, hear!

Following a successful career which took in Cae Cwm, Cae'r Bont in Abercrave, Stradey Park, Pontypool Park, St Helen's and a range of international venues, Clive's career as a player culminated in a fantastic Swansea win against Australia at St Helen's in 1966. Now that he has retired to his beloved Upper Cwmtwrch, he is a conscientious member of the Gyrlais Male Voice Choir which recently provided the pre-match entertainment at the Millennium Stadium prior to two major internationals against Australia and New Zealand. How can anyone follow that? He really has done it all!

24
6 x 6

I was nine years old when I had my first experience of international sport. The year was 1957, and my father took me to Cardiff Arms Park to see Wales play Ireland. In the summer of the same year I again found myself on a highway, but this time it was the A40, not the A48, and our destination was London. To be exact it was Lord's Cricket Ground in St John's Wood, and I was on my way to watch my first test match, England versus the West Indies.

Despite the fact that my father was sporting a new panama, we were denied access to the Members' Enclosure in front of the pavilion – in fact we were not even lucky enough to get seats in the stands. No, we were part of the orderly queue hoping and praying that we would at least gain entry to the ground.

Our patience was finally rewarded, and just as the umpires strode out onto the hallowed turf, my father and I settled down on the grass just to the left of

Sir Garfield Sobers, the greatest all-rounder of them all.

the pavilion and waited for the first ball of the day to be bowled. The team sheets for the match read like a *Who's Who* of test cricket – Rohan Kanhai, Garfield Sobers, Sonny Ramadhin, Alf Valentine, Frank Worrell, Everton Weekes, Clyde Walcott, O.G. (Collie) Smith for the West Indies while Tom Graveney, Peter May, Colin Cowdrey, Trevor Bailey, Fred Trueman and Brian Statham were to play for England. To see these players in the flesh, and at such close quarters, was a dream come true for a Welsh lad of tender years. This is what Harold Pinter had in mind when he referred to cricket as the 'greatest thing God ever created'.

Over the next five days, as we watched play unfold and wondered at the talent on display, my eye was drawn to one player in particular, and that individual was Garfield St Auburn Sobers. Even at the tender age of nineteen, he commanded respect. His undoubted ability with both bat and ball, his elegant movements about the field, all made him a focus for the thousands of pairs of eyes encircling the pitch. It was England who won the game (by an innings and 36 runs), but it was Sobers who often dominated the headlines. In a century partnership with Everton Weekes he scored 66 runs, took two wickets for a total of 28 runs and then made a spectacular catch at short leg – quite a feat for your first test match at Lord's.

As well as being my first match of international importance, this was also my first experience of witnessing a bowler with such a varied and diverse technique. One over would see him run in at speed over some twenty paces, while another would see him pose major problems for experienced batsmen like Peter May and Godfrey Evans with his deceptive spinning of the ball. Sobers was also a fantastic fielder, stalking the cover area like some caged animal, stretching in rubber-like fashion close to the bat or launching himself in the slips. The term 'all-rounder' was surely coined with Gary Sobers in mind.

Sobers had made his first appearance for the West Indies at Sabina Park, Kingston in Jamaica when he was just seventeen years of age. The game was notable on two counts – firstly that on his debut he took 4-75, and secondly that the visiting captain, Len Hutton, steered England to victory with a magnificent double century. It was Hutton who had claimed the highest individual score in a test match with 364 at the Oval in 1938 against Australia, until Sobers, at Sabina Park in 1958, scored 365 not out against Pakistan.

It is small wonder that he belongs to that elite group of sportsmen who manage to draw the crowds, simply by having their name on the team sheet. Club loyalties are temporarily abandoned as supporters turn up to appreciate the talent that is on display. In his book, *As I Said at the Time*, E.W. Swanton chronicles an amusing anecdote which illustrates this point. It involves an incident which took place at Port-of-Spain in Trinidad when a West Indies XI was playing against the touring MCC. A local barrister was determined to excuse himself from court proceedings to watch the match and would go to any lengths to do so. According to Mr Swanton:

My cuttings-book contains this choice item:

> Not even his client could have kept Mr. L.L. Roberts, solicitor, from going to the Queen's Park Oval yesterday. When his case was called, Mr. Roberts told Mr Alcindor: 'Sir, it is Hunte, Rae, Kanhai, Weekes, Walcott, Sobers, "Collie" Smith and the "Typhoon" duel, and I am asking for an adjournment in this matter.'

The adjournment was granted. A delightfully West Indian touch.

Johan Cruyff, Cristiano Ronaldo, Ryan Giggs – superstars on the football field; Nureyev and Fonteyn performing at Sadler's Wells; Nastase on the Centre Court at Wimbledon; Ayrton Senna and Juan Manuel Fangio behind the wheel of a Formula One racing car; Korbut, Comaneci and Kim in the gymnasium; Gerald Davies on the right wing and Sobers on the cricket field. These performers have one thing in common – they are natural athletes, their athleticism a part of their genetic make-up. No coach moulded any of these! As Donald Bradman once said, 'I was never coached. I was never told how to hold a bat.' Therein I suspect lies the secret of their success.

To see Gary Sobers stride out to the wicket was an experience in itself. A deathly hush would descend over the ground, coupled with an air of expectancy. All eyes followed his every movement as he approached the crease, the bat being a natural extension of his arm. As he took guard it was as if time stood still and in my mind's eye he was once again the young lad who wielded a piece of driftwood on the white beaches of the Caribbean or on the Savannah in Bridgetown. It was here that he first frustrated any aspiring young bowler as he casually hammered the ball towards the rocks or at times into the sea. Gary Sobers just oozed class.

It is fair to say that Sobers was a team in itself. The question is often asked, 'Who is the greatest cricketer of all time?' A list of illustrious names could be put forward: Bradman, Miller, Hammond, Hobbs, Richards (Barry and Viv), Botham, Tendulkar, Gavaskar, Ponting, Waugh, Hadlee, Miandad, Holding and Lillee. But the one person who could wield the most influence on the outcome of a match was, undoubtedly, Garfield Sobers.

Many renowned sports writers have waxed lyrical on the subject of cricket; none more so than Sir Neville Cardus. Indeed, one can imagine that he had the ability to turn a letter of complaint to the Gas or Electricity Board into a literary gem such was his way with words. The following extract from Wisden 1967 *The Lion of Cricket* clearly illustrates this point.

> We can safely agree that no player has proven versatility of skill as convincingly as Sobers has done, effortlessly, and after the manner born. He has boxed the compass of the world of present-day cricket, revealing his gifts easefully, abundantly. And here we touch on his secret: power of relaxation and the gift of holding himself in reserve. Nobody has seen Sobers obviously in labour. He makes a stroke with moments to spare. His fastest ball – and it

can be very fast – is bowled as though he could, with physical pressure, have bowled it a shade faster. He can, in the slips, catch the lightning snick with the grace and nonchalance of Hammond himself. The sure sign of mastery, of genius of any order, is absence of strain, natural freedom of rhythm.

I'm sure the majority of the supporters present at St Helen's on that August day in 1968 were there to see one man, and not to witness an end-of-season encounter between Glamorgan and Nottinghamshire. They had come from the Swansea, Neath, Gwendraeth, Amman and Afan valleys, from east and west Wales and beyond and all would bear witness to the remarkable achievement performed by Gary Sobers at the famous field within striking distance of Swansea Bay. For the first time in the history of the game, a batsman would hit six sixes in an over.

Always remembered as the bowler struck for six sixes but Malcolm Nash proved himself to be one of the finest new-ball bowlers in county cricket.

Nottingham had scored 308-5 when the maestro made his way to the wicket. As he did so, the bars, food stands and ice-cream vans around the ground emptied of customers. A temporary halt was called to the innumerable 'unofficial' games taking place between fathers and children on the nearby rugby field as everyone focussed on the slight figure making his way to the middle. As he negotiated the 70-odd steps from the pavilion to the meticulously tended outfield, did Sobers plan an assault on the record? In any case, within minutes he had scored 40 runs, dispatching the Glamorgan bowlers to all parts of the ground – a taste of things to come!

Facing the pavilion and with his back to the blue waters of Swansea Bay, Sobers took fresh guard to face the incoming bowler, Malcolm Nash. The first six was a stroke of majestic proportions. All eyes turned skywards as the ball soared out of the ground and came to rest against a building in Gorse Lane. The second followed in the same direction, but this time smashing a window in the nearby Cricketers Arms. There was now a buzz around the arena. As Nash ran in for the third and fourth balls of the over, spectators scrambled out of the way at long-on and midwicket respectively, as the red-leather missile hurtled in their direction. The figures for the over so far read: four balls, four sixes. The atmosphere was electric, everyone sensing that they were witnessing something quite extraordinary on a cricket ground.

The next ball from the hapless Nash was lofted in the direction of long-off where one of Glamorgan's most reliable fielders, Roger Davis, had been positioned. As was his wont, Davis caught the ball but his proximity to the boundary and the strength of the shot caused him to put his foot over the rope. Roger was the first to put up his hand and admit that the catch was null and void – five sixes! One more six would immortalise the player, the bowler and the ground!

The last ball of the over was struck with venom, right in the middle of the bat and pulled in the direction of the Brangwyn Hall, where it disappeared down a side road and was not recovered until the following day. Uproar followed as everyone took in the significance of the event. When calm was finally restored, Sobers declared the innings having scored an unforgettable 76. The following day, the name of St Helen's was heard and read worldwide.

Former India and Glamorgan all-rounder, Ravi Shastri, then equalled the feat playing for Bombay in a first class game against Baroda in 1984, and recently Herschelle Gibbs hit Daan van Bunge for six sixes in a World Cup Match at Warner Park, St Kitts in 2007. However, we in Wales cherish the fact that the feat was first achieved at St Helen's in Swansea on August 31,1968.

'Perfection is impossible, but in the pursuit of perfection we can achieve excellence.' Gary Sobers came within a hair's breadth of achieving perfection.

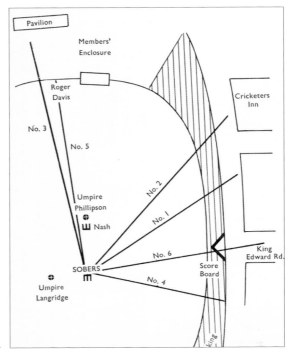

Gary Sobers's six sixes.

25
Shep

There are certain moments which are indelibly imprinted in the memory, moments which never seem to fade with time. In the annals of Welsh sport, the victories gained by Glamorgan Cricket Club against the Australian tourists in August 1964 and August 1968 were undoubtedly such events. Every now and again some sporting incidents take one's breath away, cause the heart to skip a beat; moments of such drama; moments when we can sing in chorus with Max Boyce – 'I was there!' Ever since that magnificent decade in the history of Glamorgan County Cricket Club, the purists have

Another magnificent victory against Australia in 1968. Skipper Don Shepherd celebrates along with thousands of jubilant Welshmen.

spent hours recalling and romanticising. For Don Shepherd, throughout a long and distinguished career, winning was always the only option and successive victories against the world's great exponents of the game was the ultimate accolade.

Before entering a foreign country, travellers are asked to provide certain items of information regarding their identity, date of birth, address, reasons for the visit etc. More often than not there is also a box provided under the title 'occupation'. This part of the questionnaire can often prove to be a headache – but not in Don's case. For him the answer was easy, 'Wicket taker'. He was an expert in this department, and his list of first-class wickets amounted to a staggering 2218 during 24 memorable seasons.

He was, unquestionably, the best county bowler never to have played for England. It was a travesty of justice – if he had been born within striking distance of Lord's, Old Trafford, Headingley or Edgbaston, then his fifty or more caps would have been worn with pride. He was an off-spin bowler, or perhaps an off-cutter, as he delivered the ball slightly quicker than a spinner. He captured 168 wickets in 1956, and went on to take over 100 wickets a season on a further eleven occasions, producing several extraordinary returns – 6 for 5 against Nottinghamshire, 5 for 2 against Leicestershire and 7 for 7 against Hampshire. He was also an aggressive tail-ender – a typical number 10 or 11, whose only intention was to strike the ball with venom into the next county. He entertained a capacity Bank Holiday crowd at St Helen's in 1961, scoring a half century against Australia in only eleven scoring strokes, including six sixes, three fours, a two and a single.

Cliff Davies, the Cardiff front-row forward from the village of Kenfig Hill was a real character (and such individuals are fast becoming part of folklore because of the changing nature and demands of modern sport). He loved playing on the Arms Park but was still true to his home village, a little place in Glamorgan where there's a legend that a buried city lies under the water nearby. During the 1950 Lions Tour of New Zealand and Australia, as the tour was drawing to a close, he was sorry to be losing touch with the Scots, Irish and English contingent who, until the tour, had been distant figures on the other side of the field. A coal miner, Cliff, known as 'The Bard of Kenfig Hill', was so proud of being both a miner and a son of Kenfig Hill that before the team broke up, he said, 'Well, I can't offer you much boys but if any of you would like a holiday down in Kenfig Hill, you're very welcome. There's more history attached to Kenfig Hill than any other village, town and city in the world.' The tall, elegant Peter Kininmonth, captain of Oxford University and Scotland gasped slightly. 'Well,' said Cliff, 'barring Jerusalem!'

If the Arms Park and Kenfig Hill were sacrosanct to Cliff, then Porteynon and St Helen's were God's country to the great Don Shepherd and to play in two successful Glamorgan teams in the space of four years against the Australian tourists was some accomplishment for a local lad. August Bank Holiday 1964 (which, incidentally, at that time fell on the first weekend of the month) saw all roads lead to Swansea. Two major events, one cultural, the other sporting were being held in the town on the weekend. The National Eisteddfod was staged at Singleton Park and St Helen's was playing host to the Australian cricket team. Some 40,000 or more people crowded into that small corner of South Wales on the first Saturday of August, with half of them going to enjoy the competitions at the Eisteddfod and the other half hoping to witness an exciting few days of cricket.

Neither faction would be disappointed. At St Helen's, Ossie Wheatley won the toss and elected to bat. Some questioned this decision as the weather conditions, grey and overcast, favoured the range of bowlers in Bobby Simpson's team. It seemed as if the sceptics were vindicated when Glamorgan lost two early wickets to Tom Veivers. Despite the best efforts of Peter Walker and Alan Rees, who added 68 runs for the fourth wicket, the home team fell miserably short of a decent target. The Australian fielding was fiendish in its ferocity with Simpson at slip leading by example. By mid-afternoon Glamorgan were back in the pavilion.

As was appropriate for a cricket ground situated close to the sea, the tide of fortune turned in Glamorgan's favour in the afternoon session. Australia were soon in trouble thanks to some inspired bowling by Jim Pressdee and Don

81

Shepherd. At close of play at 6.30, the visitors were 63-6 with Pressdee having taken four wickets and Shepherd two. The quality of the bowling was such that it had some of the best players in the world at sixes and sevens. Players of the calibre of Lawry, Redpath, O'Neill and Simpson – they were all finding difficulty in judging the speed and direction of the ball and were making uncharacteristic errors.

Glamorgan v. Australia, 1964.

That evening both teams were invited to join the Australian soprano Mary Collier and the Eisteddfod Choir on stage in the main pavilion. It is assumed that the cricketers did not take part in the singing, but nevertheless their presence merited a standing ovation from a capacity crowd.

When play resumed on Monday morning, Pressdee and Shepherd continued where they had left off on Saturday. They wreaked havoc amongst the Australian batsmen and the visitors were soon dismissed for 101. The rallying call in the Glamorgan changing room was for 100% concentration and 100% effort from every team member – a reasonable total was required if they were to have any chance of winning the game. However, Veivers and Simpson proved just as effective as Shep and Pressdee and the Glamorgan innings came to a close with Australia requiring 269 for victory. Alan Rees again top scored in Glamorgan's second innings and in fact was the only Glamorgan batsman to make any sort of impression.

The Australian second innings got off to a sound start with Lawry, Jarman and Veivers all making valuable contributions. But they had reckoned without the resolve of Shepherd and Pressdee. Every delivery was perfect in terms of line and length, causing a huge amount of frustration for the batsmen and forcing them to take unnecessary risks. This sense of purpose was also reflected in the Glamorgan fielding – every ball was pounced upon and Alan Rees's chest-high catch to dismiss Bill Lawry proved to be a pivotal moment in the outcome of the game. The scorecard tells its own story and, in particular, highlights the huge contribution made by the two bowlers from the Gower Peninsula – 19 wickets in three days.

Australia (Second Innings)

W.M. Lawry	c Rees b Pressdee	64
R.B. Simpson	c Walker b Shepherd	32
N.C. O'Neill	c A.R. Lewis b E.J. Lewis	14
I.R. Redpath	lbw Shepherd	5
J. Potter	b Shepherd	0
B.N. Jarman	c E.W. Jones b Pressdee	34
T.R. Veivers	b Pressdee	54
J.W. Martin	c Pressdee b Shepherd	6
R.H.D. Sellers	c Slade b Shepherd	4
N.J.N. Hawke	c E.W. Jones b Pressdee	1
A.N. Connolly	not out	0
Extras:		18
Total:		**232**

Glamorgan – bowling

	Overs	Mdns	Runs	Wickets
Wheatley	5	1	11	0
Cordle	7	1	14	0
Shepherd	52	29	71	5
Pressdee	28.1	6	65	4
E.J. Lewis	26	13	51	1
Slade	1	0	2	0

Glamorgan:	197	172
Australia:	101	232

Glamorgan won by 36 runs

When the final wicket fell to Pressdee, the crowd were ecstatic and invaded the pitch to hail the conquering heroes. The champagne flowed until dawn and on the nearby Eisteddfod field, the bards could be seen busily composing their tributes to the victorious Glamorgan XI – a team which could now claim to have beaten every major touring side.

Four years later, and almost to the day, Australia were again welcomed to St Helen's and were again comprehensively beaten by the home side. Don

Shepherd played a major role in this win also, but it was his qualities as captain that were to the fore on this occasion. Glamorgan won the toss and elected to bat. A total of 224 (Alan Jones 99, Majid Khan 55) was deemed reasonable on a wicket which favoured medium-pace bowling. Malcolm Nash was having a red-letter day with the ball, and his figures of 5-28 were a reflection of the accuracy of his bowling. Australia were dismissed for 110.

More celebrations as the Aussies are beaten in 1968.

In their second innings the Glamorgan batsmen Roger Davis (59), Brian Davis (66) and Alan Rees (33 not out) all contributed to a fine total of 250-9 dec. – Barry Jarman's team required 364 for victory. Don Shepherd's captaincy was inspirational – encouraging, praising, cajoling and keeping faith with his bowlers when things did not go quite according to plan. One who benefited from this approach was the spinner, Brian Lewis – when many would have relegated the bowler of one or two expensive overs to patrolling the boundary rope, Shep kept faith. The result was that Lewis ended the match with a tally of seven wickets.

Without doubt, the turning point in the game came with the dismissal of Paul Sheahan. The young batsman was on 137 and gaining in confidence. A delivery from Peter Walker was struck in the middle of the bat and was climbing over the bowler's head on its way to the boundary. Like a jack-in-the-box, Walker sprung into the air and, with arm outstretched, intercepted the ball in mid-flight, before falling on his back onto the grass with the ball safely in his grasp.

For an instant, the ground fell silent in disbelief – Sheahan was rooted to the spot, incredulous at what he had just witnessed. Glamorgan went on to win the match by 79 runs and, as happened four years earlier, the crowd invaded the pitch with scenes of jubilation all around St Helen's. This had been a very successful decade in the history of Glamorgan CCC – two wins against the Australians and winners of the County Championship, and no one had played a bigger part in this success than D.J. Shepherd.

26
Majid Khan

As fanatical as he was about sport, my father Len Bevan was also an unusual fan. Ever since he was a young man he was drawn to talented individuals rather than particular teams. Consequently, as a lad, I got to know Wales well by travelling to the most obscure places. How many other seven-year-olds from west Wales frequented the sporting grounds of Newbridge, Ebbw Vale, Pontypridd, Penarth and Cross Keys on a regular basis? If Onllwyn Brace was playing for Newport in Pandy Park, the car would take us to the remote Sirhowy Valley; if D. Ken Jones and Brian Davies were running riot at

Majid Jehangir Khan on the attack. A ferocious straight drive.

Ynysangharad Park, we'd journey through Aberdare and Mountain Ash to Pontypridd; we'd often tour Gwent to witness Bryan Richards and Dewi Bebb playing for the All Whites, and, at times, if Cyril Davies and Barry John were playing for Cardiff, we'd even contemplate crossing Offa's Dyke. Undoubtedly, if my father was as fit and agile today, he'd be racing up and down the M4 to appreciate the skills of players like Shane Williams, James Hook, Dwayne Peel, Regan King, Kevin Morgan, Michael Owen and Martyn Williams.

Like father, like son. Often in the past, my attendance at various games has been decided by the individuals playing rather than the teams concerned. Some years ago I spent an educational hour-and-a-half at the Bernabeu in Madrid, appreciating an amazing performance by Zinadine Zidane – I can't remember the exact score between Real Madrid and Real Mallorca, as it was the Frenchman's incredible skill that demanded my attention. I am still captivated by those images of him controlling the action with such apparent ease. Similarly, a visit to the United Centre in Chicago during the late 1990s was determined by my ambition to witness Michael Jordan's breathtaking performance, as opposed to any loyalty to the Chicago Bulls. Again, I was mesmerised by the American giant's confident domination of the basketball court.

Despite being a keen supporter of Tony Lewis's Glamorgan team during the late 1960s, there was another reason for getting up early and travelling to St Helen's. If you were to ask me to name my favourite cricketers from the past, there'd be a number of Glamorgan and Caribbean players on that list, and it would read as follows: Alan Jones, Allan Watkins, Don Shepherd, Michael Holding, Everton Weekes, Gary Sobers, Viv Richards, Graham Pollock, Barry

Richards and Brian Lara, but the number-one spot must go to that cricketing genius from Pakistan, Majid Khan. To watch him play was a truly incredible experience. Whatever the state of the game, Majid would stroll out to the crease in an apparently nonchalant manner, as if he were taking a leisurely morning or afternoon stroll. Nothing intimidated him. He resembled more of the West Indian character – laid-back, sporting a well-worn pair of shabby pads and threadbare gloves and occasionally donning a sun hat, which looked like something his great-grandfather had bought in the early twentieth century at some Asian bazaar.

As he made his way down those steps at St Helen's, his manner contrasted sharply with those other batsmen who found the long walk itself nerve-wracking, and showed it by fidgeting with their gloves, bat, pads etc. Once he had reached the wicket, Majid, conscious of the fact that all eyes were focussed on

Graceful and destructive.

him, would take guard. He would take an over or so to get used to the conditions, judge the pace of the wicket, the bowler's line etc, and then you knew that at any moment he would explode into action.

The slightest bowling error would be pounced on instantly and the ball dispatched to all corners of the ground. He had the eyes and radar of a falcon, a fatal combination for an inept bowler. A naturally gifted batsman, he had the ability to score quickly and effortlessly. I shall never forget his cover drive, as graceful a shot as you would ever wish to see – often dancing to the pitch off the ball and readjusting the ball's direction as it sped like a rocket to the boundary rope. When faced with a short ball, he'd instinctively step back, striking the ball in the meat of the bat, helping it on its way to the far reaches of the ground. His strength was legendary and made him an excellent fielder – a powerful arm enabling him to throw the ball low, like a torpedo, into the wicketkeeper's gloves. I'm not sure whether wicketkeeper Eifion Jones was always pleased about this!

On Tuesday, August 8, 1967, Majid Jehangir Khan was immortalised as a result of a performance which won him a place in the St Helen's hall of cricketing fame. It was the last day of a rain-affected contest between Glamorgan and Pakistan – Tony Lewis decided to close the Glamorgan first innings and challenge the visiting team. The visitors were soon in trouble, two wickets fell cheaply but then the dangerous duo, Saeed and Majid, increased the tempo and entertained the expectant crowd. 215 runs came in 89 minutes; Majid hit 100 in 61 minutes, including 5 sixes in one over off Roger Davis and 17 sixes in a sparkling 147 not out. Rain curtailed play with Glamorgan 72 for 2 requiring 324 to win.

The Welsh county's spectators and management committee were bowled over. Majid's breathtaking cameo is still talked about by everyone privileged to have been there. There was, obviously, an attempt to coax and cajole the captain Saeed Ahmed – Glamorgan desperately wanted a declaration in order to try to win the game. However, even taking this into account, Majid's performance was still pretty awesome. As a result of this act of wanton destruction, he was approached by the county, agreed terms and returned to Wales the following season as one of Glamorgan's overseas players. The decision proved inspirational. Within two years Tony Lewis's team were crowned county champions for the second time in their history with Majid Khan a vital and inspirational team member.

27

Whites against the Whites

by Peter Hain

'I voted for you, Peter, but you spoilt my Saturday that time against the Springboks,' Neath constituents would often tell me when I was first elected their MP in 1991.

The 'my Saturday' referred to was of course mid-November 1969 when the white South Africans played against the All Whites. Early in their 25-match tour, which was heavily disrupted by pitch invasions and other direct-action protests, the match saw bitter clashes between spectators and demonstrators who had entered St Helen's to try to stop play.

The trouble started when over 2,000 anti-apartheid demonstrators marched on the ground, clashing with police and triggering what was later described as one of 'the worst incidents of mob violence in Britain since the 1930s.' South Wales police constabulary colluded with rugby 'vigilantes' to attack the non-violent protesters.

The worst incidents took place inside the ground where, just after half-time, about 100 demonstrators invaded the pitch and peacefully sat down, stopping the match for over five minutes. Stewards and police immediately started attacking them, young women and men alike. After being dragged off, some were thrown back into more vociferous sections of the St Helen's crowd where they were beaten again.

Afterwards, a group of Reading University students took the coach home, demoralised and in shock, one with a broken jaw and in danger of losing an eye, another having been dragged off by his genitals and then repeatedly assaulted by spectators.

Impartial observers and journalists condemned the violence of these rugby supporters and police. On November 22, John Jones, who played for Swansea in 1939, was reported in the *Guardian* to be dissociating himself from the Welsh Rugby Union in disgust after seeing 'suede-jacketed toffs acting like thugs and bullying demonstrators'. At St Helen's, he said, he saw a former player he knew pull a girl 30 yards by her hair. Later in a local hotel, he 'heard the stewards openly boasting about it as they caroused with the Springboks'.

There were demands in Parliament for the Home Secretary

Bitter clashes between police, spectators and protesters at St Helen's in 1969.

89

to order a public inquiry. As chairman of the Stop the Tour campaign, I led a delegation to the Home Office complaining that 'this private army of rugby thugs was responsible for some of the most systematic and brutal mob violence ever seen on peaceful demonstrators in Britain.' Unless something was done to curb the actions of 'vigilantes', I said, 'someone may get killed' during the remaining twenty matches of the tour.

The passions for watching rugby on one side and opposing apartheid on the other could not be reconciled. At the time, the two sides came to despise each other with a vengeance. Some (like me as it happens) could be both rugby fans and anti-apartheid militants. Carwyn James, the Llanelli coach, supported us. So did John Taylor, of London Welsh, Wales and the British Lions, who refused to play against the Springboks. But overwhelmingly, the two sides glared angrily at each other across police lines in mutual incomprehension, a clash of cultures, generations, and often politics too. For us, it was a question of morality and a fierce anti-racism. For them the game came first, always.

I was unable to persuade ardent rugby fans that because the Springboks were selected from the minority white population, they did not truly represent South Africa. That because schoolboy rugby players (like I had been) were not permitted by apartheid to play each other across the colour divide, and clubs were rigidly segregated, rugby in South Africa during those grim days was not really rugby as we knew and loved it in South Wales, it was *apartheid rugby* and we should have nothing to do with it.

In the event, the campaign triggered a worldwide boycott of white South African sports teams. As Nelson Mandela told me many years later, it proved a decisive blow against the evil tyranny of apartheid. It had not just left him and his comrades languishing in a cold prison cell on Robben Island (and had forced my parents and family to leave for Britain in 1966), but prevented blacks from becoming Springboks.

By the time I was elected Neath MP in 1991, passions had cooled. Nelson Mandela's release from 10,000 days in prison had forced a re-think amongst even our strongest critics. Many rugby fans, who had hated me for years after the Stop the Tour campaign I led, have since gone out of their way to tell me that they now understood the reasons for it.

Nevertheless one disagreement steadfastly remained. 'I carried you off the pitch that day,' my constituents repeatedly told me. 'I wasn't even there!' I replied.

But, after dozens had proudly made the same claim, refusing to accept my protestations that I was actually up in London receiving telephone calls from badly beaten friends and fellow protesters, I stopped trying to deny it. Why spoil a bit of folklore for the facts? After all, it meant scores of local rugby fans could still regale their local rugby club bars about how they proudly threw their MP out of St Helen's that Saturday afternoon in 1969.

Peter Hain is MP for Neath and was first appointed Secretary of State for Wales in 2002. He spent his childhood in South Africa when his parents were jailed, banned, prevented from earning a living, and finally forced to leave for Britain.

28
The David Parkhouse Memorial Match

International XV
v.
Combined Penclawdd, Llanelli and Swansea XV

David Parkhouse, or Dai to his friends, was a giant. He must have been one of the tiniest rugby players to have worn the All Whites jersey but he possessed the heart of a lion, and was always full of trickery. Dai started his playing career at Penclawdd and was full of praise for the opportunities provided by the local team. Smaller village clubs were in the main nursery units, nurturing the talents of young players and preparing them both physically and mentally for that step up to the higher echelons of the game.

Dai, together with his great friend Bryan Richards, thrilled the Swansea faithful in the early 1960s. He was the embodiment of cheeky, carefree athleticism and, according to Len Blyth, the former Welsh international,

Dai Parkhouse : heart of a lion.

possibly one of the the pioneers of the 'no kicking between the two twenty-fives' law. In a moving tribute in the memorial match programme, Mr Blyth reminds us of Dai's wizardry in the 1963 Swansea v. New Zealand match. 'Undeterred by waves of All Black forwards, including Meads, Tremain, Graham and Gray, the Swansea fullback constantly appeared from ruck and maul complete with ball in hand, a huge grin on his face ready to take on the might of the whole All Black side.'

Terry McLean, the renowned New Zealand rugby critic, who very rarely praises All Black opponents, wrote this about Dai after the above match. 'Welsh rugby is indeed in good hands when it can produce players with such skill and guts as the diminutive Dai Parkhouse, who gave a display to swell the hearts of Welshmen and amazed our boys by his full-blooded tackling, and capped it all by scoring nine points, two penalty goals and one dropped goal – the highest individual contribution against the touring side during the 1963/64 tour.' I was present at St Helen's on that freezing December Saturday in 1963 – Wilson Whineray's men were deserved winners 16-9, but everyone that evening was talking about the man from Penclawdd, who was the undoubted man of the match.

Ron Griffiths, the rugby correspondent of *The South Wales Evening Post* was just as complimentary: 'If Oscars were awarded in rugby football, David Parkhouse would surely have picked up a hatful. For, above all else, he was an entertainer, a player who breathed the true spirit of rugby football . . . He used to pop up in all sorts of unexpected places to create general confusion in the ranks of the opposition. He injected adventure into the game and so endeared himself to rugby-lovers wherever he appeared. At St Helen's he will always be remembered as the cheeky chappie, always bubbling over with enthusiasm.'

The untimely death of Dai Parhhouse robbed the game of one of its greatest characters. On Thursday, April 9, 1970, the David Parkhouse Memorial Match was staged at St Helen's as a tribute to a truly great rugby player.

International XV: Barry John, Allan Lewis, Brian Davies, J.P.R. Williams, Ian Hall, Wynne Davies, Gareth Edwards, John Lloyd, John Young, Gareth Rees, Delme Thomas, Brian Thomas, Dai Morris, Mervyn Davies, John Taylor.

Combined XV: Doug Rees, Roy Mathias, Arwel Rees, Alan Parkhouse (c), Stuart Davies, John Evans, Selwyn Williams, Mel James, Roy Thomas, Paul Jones, Stuart Gallagher, Jeff Roberts, Ken Lewis, Robert Morgan, Hywel Gravelle.

Referee: Ivor Morgan
Touch Judges: Dennis Parkhouse, Morlais Davies

They came in their thousands to pay tribute to the charismatic Gower man, and to see some of the nation's greats playing with a panache that Dai himself would have endorsed. And it was a classic, both teams full of enterprise for an hour and twenty minutes. Dai would have relished reading the back pages the morning after, realising that Barry, Gareth, J.P.R., Dai, Merv, Delme and John Taylor had all accepted an invitation to entertain in the spirit intended by William Webb Ellis in the nineteenth century, and Dai himself in the 1960s.

The crowd was, however, electrified by the genius of one individual above all others. His name was Barry John. He played out of position, at fullback, that evening, safe in the knowledge that he wouldn't be facing a barrage of garryowens chased down by warrior forwards. He wouldn't either be expected to tackle aggressively or fall manfully on loose ball. From first to last, the tactics would be all-out counter-attack – from his own half, from his own 22, and even from behind his own line. He entered the three-quarter line time and again, sometimes appearing at the fly half's shoulder, sometimes haring up outside the wingers, or popping up for an inside pass from his centres. He was a combination of George Nepia, Lewis Jones, Serge Blanco and ... Dai Parkhouse. The Penclawdd fullback couldn't have been paid a more eloquent tribute.

> **International XV** 49 (Barry John try, two conversions; Allan Lewis 2 tries; Brian Davies try, conversion; J.P.R. Williams try; Wynne Davies try; Jeff Young 2 tries; Mervyn Davies try; John Taylor try, 4 conversions; Dai Morris try, conversion).

> **Combined XV** 26 (Alan Parkhouse try; Stuart Davies try; John Evans try; Jeff Roberts try; Ken Lewis try; Hywel Gravelle try; Doug Rees 4 conversions).

St. Helen's Ground, Swansea

THURSDAY, APRIL 9th, 1970

DAVID PARKHOUSE MEMORIAL MATCH

INTERNATIONAL XV

v.

COMBINED PENCLAWDD, LLANELLI AND SWANSEA XV

Kick-off 7.0 p.m.   Programme 1/-

29
Please Admit to Test Match

David Green was a contemporary of Tony Lewis and the *Daily Telegraph* journalist (who opened the batting for Gloucestershire and Lancashire) described the Glamorgan and England captain as a shrewd, knowledgeable and inventive skipper. *The Guardian* reporter Frank Keating reminds us that this was not always so!

Fred Trueman never toured India with England. Tony Lewis did, as captain, in 1972. He was a marvellously civil, genteel, humorous and much-loved leader. In India you have to be; they worship cricket. Five hundred autographs a day is the norm for a visiting net bowler. Lewis would sign his name into the night. One day, at Bangalore or Kanpur, or wherever, a man knocked on his door each hour of the day prior to the Test Match – 'My dear uncle, Lewis-sahib, please sign these sheets of paper for my big and beloved family!'

Tony would readily and dutifully sign each proffered piece 'A.R. Lewis'. By the second day of the Test, a gateman at last felt himself duty-bound to approach the England captain. Surely he had been too profligate with his invitations. Every sheet Tony had signed had been topped and tailed with the typewritten legend 'Please admit to Test Match. Signed: A.R. Lewis, captain of England'.

Tony Lewis – Glamorgan's inspirational captain in their Championship-winning season in 1969.

30
The Italian Job

by David Protheroe

Having played my first game for the club in the previous season, I was delighted to hear that as part of our preparations for the 1972/73 season, we were to visit Rome. This was a short pre-season tour to play two games, the first against a select XV and the other versus the full-blown Italian side.

We arrived safely and set up camp under the watchful eye of our coach Ieuan Evans in the village used for the 1960 Olympic Games. This was an experience in itself but, as I was to shortly find out, this trip was to teach me much more than I had bargained for. Luckily I was selected for the first encounter at outside half, with my student colleague and competitor for the pivot role, Dai Richards, in the centre partnering the excellent Darrell Cole. This meant that the usual outside centre, Arwel Rees (alias Zac) had been rested. Well, we won the match comfortably enough, although we had not reached the heights that we had hoped.

So it was off to the city to celebrate, with my minder Colin Davies, known to one and all as Tally Bach, promising all sorts of things! Following an excellent banquet with our hosts, we decamped to one of those stylish Italian corner bars, you know something like Crescis in Gwauncaegurwen, except that the square it stood on was nearly the size of the Waun. As the wine flowed, so did the inevitable discussions on team selection and, from one particular corner, it was maintained that Zac, obviously, should have played. The incessant plea grew louder and became quite a nuisance, whereupon, and in the interest of team morale, our incomparable captain, Mel James, decided to sort it! The offending player was helped outside, cuffed by Mel, and lay comatose upon the cobbled Roman square.

Then all hell broke loose. There were Vespas and Italian youths everywhere under the misapprehension that we had laid out one of their own. The next fifteen minutes can only be described as mayhem as we sought to defend ourselves. I was agog eating a Mars bar as all this went on. Suddenly blue lights were flashing and the Carabinieri surrounded us. There was no other option but to leg it! It's at this juncture that it is said that Dai Richards perfected his sidestep dodging the bullets.

Anyway, I was pursued up a side street by one of the police cars, which swerved across the pavement in front of me, resulting in my cartwheeling over the bonnet. By this time, the charismatic prop Neil Webb had caught up and I thought he'd said 'Resist them, Dai,' so I did. A big mistake . . . as they laid into me with fists and rifle butts. As one towered over me with the gun barrel in my chest making clicking noises like the Lone Ranger, Webby was shouting 'Don't resist them, Dai, don't resist them for goodness' sake!'

So before we knew it, both of us were in the aptly-named Queen of Heaven Penitentiary, shortly to be joined by Roger Hyndman, John Roberts and Tally Bach who greeted me with the immortal words – 'See, Dai, I told you I'd be here to look after you!' We were all taken to separate cells, sharing with local inmates; mine stank! We tried to communicate with one another as the Italians goaded us, shouting 'Pugno Pugno!' Webby tried valiantly to raise morale, informing us that the bingo cards would be round shortly.

Next morning the British Embassy envoys came to see us – progress at last. 'Don't worry, Mr Protheroe, we will bring you fresh pyjamas and toiletries weekly.'

What do you think this is, a holiday camp?' I retorted. 'Get me out of here!'

'Well, it's not that easy. You see, two of the policemen are in hospital with broken jaws. It could be anything from six months to two years.' Mam fach! Speaking of whom, I don't think she ever got over it as apparently the first she knew of it was reading the front page of the *Western Mail* in the morning and passing out in shock. It certainly created a stir in Rhiwfawr.

Well, fortunately, after just over a week of pasta and raw eggs, a top lawyer convinced the court that it made sense to extradite us from the country rather than use up Italian taxes to keep us in prison. So we were whisked away as quickly as we has arrived in jail, and I for one was pleased to say 'Arrivederci Roma'.

Some 25 years later, I returned and, following a Wales v. Italy international, I was walking across this square with my friend Stuart Griffith (Chico). And it suddenly dawned on me, almost like déjà vu, that this was the square where it had all happened. I turned to Chico and said, 'For goodness' sake, don't eat a Mars bar here, whatever you do!'

Post script:

Colin Davies (Tally Bach) from Amman United was involved in a memorable Swansea v. Barbarians encounter in 1972, memorable because the All Whites played with only fourteen men for all but fifteen minutes of the first half. Alan Meredith, the Swansea scrum half, was injured and carried off and in pre-replacement days, Colin Davies, with his flowing red locks, moved up from fullback to take his place. This was his first appearance at scrum half but he played magnificently in an unexpected 27-25 victory for the home side. With four tries apiece, Phil Llewellyn's team clinched victory with a penalty goal four minutes from time, kicked by one David Protheroe. It had been my chance to help out Tally Bach!

31
Alan Jones

Youngsters these days aren't happy unless they are sporting the latest designer gear. Whatever sport they participate in, the clothes, the equipment and even the bag to carry it in must display the appropriate logo. Back in the 1940s, things were a little different in the Jones household in Felindre, a small village on the outskirts of Swansea. As one of a family of eleven children (nine brothers and two sisters), Alan Jones was not overly familiar with brand names such as Gunn and Moore, Stuart Surridge, Duncan Fearnley and Gray Nicholls. Rather, when the boys played cricket on a bumpy strip in a nearby field, the 'bats' they used were pieces of wood lovingly prepared by either their father, or the Reverend Walter Jones, the minister of the local chapel.

These cricket matches were hotly contested affairs – no brotherly love was on display here! In fact, the term 'sibling rivalry' could have been coined in the Jones household. There was great excitement one summer when the local council decided to lay a strip of concrete right outside the family home. The brothers felt as if Christmas had arrived early. At last they had somewhere decent where they could play the game. Unfortunately, their excitement was short lived. Within a couple of months, Pontardawe Rural District Council's heavy traction equipment and steam rollers had moved in ready to tarmacadam the road. Their beloved piece of concrete was reduced to a fine powder, and so it was back to the neighbouring meadow. The surface here was so uneven that according to Alan, 'Bradman himself would have struggled!'

Although itself not a cricketing paradise, Felindre was surrounded by villages with more than adequate facilities where anyone with an interest in the sport could indulge their passion. At fourteen years of age, and now the proud owner of a Gunn and Moore bat, Alan started attending the nets at Waverley Park in nearby Clydach. The coaches there, Fred Samways, Glan Davies, Wat Jones and Oliver Williams, were so impressed with the youngster's natural ability that they almost immediately referred him to the Glamorgan Indoor School at Neath.

What was most surprising was that no one had actually taught Alan the technique of holding a bat, or how to move his feet into position – these things seemed to come naturally. What was needed now was the fine tuning to get him to play at the highest level. Although he was steadfast in his resolve to better himself, there were still occasions when his nerves got the better of him. He even started to question his own ability.

However, there were no such doubts in George Levis's mind. Levis was the Glamorgan coach in charge at Neath and, on his recommendation, the invitation came to join Glamorgan County Cricket Club. The year was 1954, and it was still the era when young men had to complete their National

Glamorgan's finest : opening batsman, Alan Jones.

Service. Also, at the start of the 1950s, a journey from west Wales to Cardiff along the A48 was a major event in a teenager's life. Nevertheless, Alan persevered and spent several seasons travelling back and forth to the nets in the North Stand of the Arms Park in Cardiff. Under the guidance of George Levis and Phil Clift, the raw talent was being finely honed. Being a professional cricketer requires a highly competitive edge and a strong mental attitude to be able to succeed in what can, at times, be a cruel sport – and there were some who questioned whether Alan had the necessary qualities.

As if the hours spent in Cardiff were not stressful enough, he would then spend an hour or more perfecting his technique on the road outside his house. Here he would practice his stance against imaginary spin and fast bowling, cutting off the back foot and driving off the front foot in turn. His brothers devised an ingenious method of helping him follow through – an empty tin was hung on a piece of string from a nearby elderberry tree and if he struck the tin then he had executed the shot correctly.

Like so many of his peers, Alan enrolled in the armed forces. After a ten-week stint of training at Maindee Barracks, he was ready for his posting overseas. The news came that he was on his way to Benghazi in Libya, but a few days before they were about to leave, Alan was summoned to see the duty sergeant.

'Jones, you need to telephone the Glamorgan Cricket Office, reverse the charges and ask to speak to Mr Wooller,' was the instruction.

Alan slowly dialled 29956.

'Skip, it's Alan Jones. You wanted to speak to me? I'm on my way to Africa.'

'No, you're not,' was the immediate reply. 'Do you want to go?'

'Well, not really – they don't play cricket in the Sahara!'

Alan's confidence was beginning to rise – maybe he could stay home after all.

'Leave it with me,' said the Glamorgan captain.

Mr Wooller was a formidable character at the best of times and the thought of a run-in with a member of the armed forces posed no threat to him. A few days later, Private Jones was again summoned – this time to see his Commanding Officer, a Major Stephenson.

'Jones, Wilfred Wooller has been in touch. He wants you to stay in Wales. I've agreed to his request with one condition – if you stay you'll have to play a few games for us and the Combined Services. Oh, and Jones – unless you score a few runs, you're on your way to North Africa!' Fortunately, for all concerned, Private Jones amassed a few hundred runs during the time and travelled no further south than Portsmouth!

One of Alan Jones's childhood heroes was the Australian left-handed batsman, Neil Harvey. It is ironic that Alan's first appearance with Glamorgan was in a game played at St Helen's against the Australian tourists in 1953. Aficionados of the game maintain that Harvey's innings of 180 (c Parkhouse b W.E. Jones) was a text-book example of how to bat – an innings still talked about by those present. It certainly was a majestic batting performance. Alan was twelfth man for the game and was called upon to patrol the mid-off area for a few overs. Within a few deliveries, he was called upon to field a firm shot from Harvey's bat – an unbelievable moment for the new recruit and still treasured by the man from Felindre. His boyhood hero was, after all, Neil Harvey!

The Australians were again the visitors at St Helen's in the summer of 1968. Having lost to the Welsh county here in 1964, Barry Jarman's team was not about to let history repeat itself again four years on. But that is precisely what happened. Thanks to an outstanding performance, scoring 99 in a total of 224 in the first innings and sharing a fourth-wicket partnership of 84 with Majid Khan, Alan Jones played an integral role in enabling Don Shepherd's team to beat the Australians by 79 runs. The victory was the more remarkable considering that the wicket favoured the spin and medium-paced bowlers of the team from down under. Jones mastered both the bowlers and the conditions.

Roy Fredericks and Alan Jones shared a record opening partnership of 330 against Northamptonshire at St Helen's in 1972. (This was broken by Matthew Elliott and Steve James at Colwyn Bay in 2000.)

Another match at St Helen's at the end of August 1972 was surely a high point in the career of two of its participants – one from Berbice in Guyana and the other from Felindre in Glamorgan. The visitors for this championship match were Northamptonshire, who were bowled out for 300 on the first day of play (Roger Davis taking 5-55). Alan Jones and his sometimes volatile opening partner, Roy Fredericks, then began the Glamorgan reply. In what was to become a record-breaking opening partnership for the Welsh county, Alan Jones scored 105 before being bowled by John Steele, while Fredericks went on to score an unbeaten 228 before Tony Lewis declared at 346-2.

The sizeable crowd enjoyed calypso cricket not often witnessed at St Helen's. Fredericks was firing on all cylinders with the ball being dispatched with venom to all corners of the ground. Jones on the other hand was playing the more cautious game, waiting for an overpitched or short ball before taking advantage. The two complemented each other perfectly – the first-wicket partnership realised 330 runs. Both players received a standing ovation but, despite their best efforts, Glamorgan still managed to lose the match. They needed 247 for victory but were 29 runs short of the target – Bedi and Cottam taking the wickets.

Of all the wonderful innings (and there were many) that Alan Jones played at St Helen's, one in particular stands out. I shall never forget Jones and his partner Bernard Hedges make that long walk down the steps from the pavilion to the square, heads bowed, deep in thought as they contemplated what lay ahead. What had they had to face was the speed and ferocity of the two fastest bowlers in the world at that time – the West Indian quickies Wes Hall and Charlie Griffith. There were no protective helmets and the like in those days, and the thought of facing up to one or two balls from either of those bowlers was enough to get the adrenalin going and dramatically increase the heart rate.

Alan was on a high. Having scored an unbeaten 104 in the previous day's encounter with Essex, he was ready for the challenge. And rise to the occasion he did with a superbly grafted innings of 161 not out. His cover drives, pulls, square cuts, late cuts, straight drives were all in evidence as he delighted a huge Swansea crowd.

Fast-forward to September 2003 and a game against Pontarddulais 1st XI. Now a 'senior citizen' and in his sixties he still managed to compile a majestic 84 showing to the youngsters playing against him that class will always out. He played in one unofficial test match for England against the Rest of the World in 1970 – he should have been a regular for a decade or more. Great man; great player.

32
Catches win Matches!

Once the cricket season started, the journey from Brynaman to St Helen's was our monthly pilgrimage. We came to worship our heroes – Parkhouse, Hedges, Watkins, Shepherd and Pressdee – in awe of their wizardry with bat and ball. But for all the graceful strokeplay of the batsmen and the accuracy and trickery of the bowlers, there were other more dramatic delights to behold in the field. Indeed, some of the acrobatics performed by many of the fielders could easily have been transferred to the circus on the neighbouring recreation round. Alan Rees, Allan Watkins, Willie Jones, Jim Pressdee, Gilbert Parkhouse, Billy Slade, Jim McConnon, Wilfred Wooller and the master of them all, Peter Walker, were some of the best fielders in the game.

In recent times, radio and television commentators have been at pains to stress how important it is to have a good fielding side if a team is to be successful. A dropped catch here, a misfield there, has in many instances cost a

One of the world's greatest ever fieldsmen; the incomparable Peter Walker.

side the match. Players of the calibre of Jonty Rhodes, Colin Bland, Paul Sheahan, Derek Randall, Tony Lock, Bobby Simpson, Mickey Stewart, Garfield Sobers, Vivian Richards, Roger Harper, Clive Lloyd, Trevor Penny, Anthony Cottey, Matthew Maynard, and Phil Sharpe have all contributed to raising the standard of fielding in cricket, whether this be close to the wicket or policing the boundary rope. While there may be more emphasis on fitness and training in the modern game, one has to remember that the Glamorgan players of the 1960s and 1970s could hold their own in any situation and compare favourably with their modern-day counterparts.

On a recent visit to Hamilton in New Zealand, I found myself scanning the shelves in a second-hand bookshop, where I came across a book written by Bobby Simpson – himself a master in the slip cordon. In one piece, the former Australian captain and opening batsman was extolling the virtues of those he considered the best fielders of his generation. Having given several examples, it was heartening to read that one of the best catches Simpson had ever witnessed was the one made by Billy Slade off the bowling of Don Shepherd at St Helen's in 1964 (a game which Glamorgan won by 36 runs).

However, as someone who is always compiling lists of 'ten best . . .', my pantheon of best fielders would always have Peter Walker in the No.1 slot. In my opinion he was the best leg-side fielder ever to have played the game – a genius. Of course his physique gave him that extra edge; he was tall and lanky but his lightning-quick reactions proved the downfall of many a batsman. A ball destined to land near the boundary rope often ended up much closer to the wicket in the palm of Walker's hands. One had to feel sorry for the bemused batsman who looked on incredulously before, head bowed, beginning the long walk back to the pavilion. The authoritative Walker often reminded me of Zebedee in the popular children's series *The Magic Roundabout*.

To field at St Helen's was a joy – the playing surface having been lovingly tended by the master groundsman George Clement. It was said that George could be seen on his knees, magnifying glass in hand, daring a weed to poke its head hrough the grass. One of the Glamorgan players who took full advantage of the playing conditions at Swansea was Alan Rees, the multi-

Alan Rees, patrolled the cover area like a restless panther.

talented ball player who played at outside half for Wales before signing professional terms with Leeds Rugby League Football Club. His favoured fielding position was in the covers, from where he would pounce on the ball like some predatory animal. The smoothness of the grass meant that he could bend, scoop up the ball and throw it into the wicketkeeper in one fluid movement, a joy to behold. This, coupled with the fact that he had a throwing action resembling a catapult, meant that the ball had landed in David Evans or Eifion Jones's gloves before the batsman had drawn breath. The result was that many a batsman would be run out after hitting what they confidently believed was a run-making stroke. There really is more to cricket than just being good with a bat or ball!

Another unbelievable fielder, who impressed the enthusiastic Brynaman schoolboys who boarded the double decker in the good old 1950s, was Allan Watkins. Alun Rees in *Welsh Sporting Greats* states that 'Watkins was the glory of Glamorgan's leg trap and the despair of physicists. He wrecked every law of aerodynamics. A body moving through the air, this branch of science insists, is subject to drag. That's why they make fast things pointy. Watkins was never pointy. He was, to be blunt, blunt. Just as well: any quicker and he'd have been catching blokes before they got to the wicket. At short fine leg, he was unsurpassable.'

Immaculate timing, a feature of Allan Watkins's batting.

104

Such great figures inspired those less gymnastic members of the team too, which is why we end this piece with the unlikely figure of Ossie Wheatley, a vital member of Glamorgan's Championship-winning team of 1969. It would not be unkind to say that Wheatley was not the most athletic of cricketers – in fact he was quite cumbersome around the field and never fleet of foot. However, he had a very good right arm, as he demonstrated with great aplomb in a vital championship match against Essex at St Helen's towards the end of the 1969 season. Glamorgan desperately needed a win, the match was closely contested and Essex required just three runs to win with just one wicket remaining. Ray East glided the ball in the direction of Wheatley fielding on the third-man boundary. They easily completed the first run and came back for the second but the opening bowler, boasting a thick mane of peroxide-coloured hair, darted in majestically and in one movement threw in. East and Lever were in the process of crossing for a second run (which would have tied the match) but they had reckoned without Mr Wheatley's pinpoint accuracy. The Essex man was run out and Glamorgan had won a thrilling contest by a solitary run.

33
Merv the Swerve

I felt as if I already knew Mervyn Davies years before he first played for Wales and then went on to become an international star. This familiarity with the back-row forward stemmed from the many anecdotes told by Bleddyn Jones with whom I had shared my youth in Brynaman. Bleddyn, who represented the Leicester Tigers on 333 occasions in the 1970s, played against Mervyn at schoolboy level and then alongside side him when the two were at Swansea College of Education. As Bleddyn recalls:

'Entering my first training session as a fresher at Swansea College of Education in the autumn of 1966, the tall, lean figure of the fresh-faced Mervyn Davies (no sign of the trademark bristling bandit moustache) stood out amongst the gathering throng. I instantly recognised him as we had crossed paths before at our respective secondary schools. Amman Valley Grammar School was expected to make short thrift of the opposition from the Swansea-based Penlan Comprehensive School. It was far from being the case as we just scraped through to win the games due to the fact that we were playing against a one-man team, and that man was Thomas Mervyn Davies. He ran, tackled, commanded the line-out and caused mayhem amongst the Amman Valley ranks.

Mervyn Davies at a Welsh training session, alongside Derek Quinnell, Gareth Edwards and Malcolm Lewis.

'So, a year or so later, it was with the utmost respect for the man that I lined up alongside him in the College XV. He was outstanding week in, week out. Merv was a vital cog in the team, his performances were outstanding, he enjoyed his rugby immensely but showed no inclination that he had any ambitions to reach the higher echelons of the game. As well as playing rugby, Merv was also a very good basketball player, representing the college in the Welsh Colleges Basketball team. This of course helped him in the lines-out when we were back on the rugby field where he would, incidentally, be our only representative in the Welsh Colleges Rugby team. Much to everyone's disbelief, the powers-that-be at Swansea RFC failed to recognise his talents. The All Whites were not enjoying the best of times during the 1960s and they could have done with Merv's presence in the team. In the end he made one appearance for the senior side when he was selected to play for them over the Christmas period.

Gareth Edwards scores against Ireland as Merv (with headband) looks on.

'On the morning of the Wales v. Scotland encounter in February 1968, Swansea College played their customary local derby against our great rivals Carmarthen Trinity College at Ashleigh Road in Swansea. As usual, the game was very physical and Merv was forced to leave the field halfway through the second half. At the end of the game, he made his way to the nearby hospital for an X-ray (which revealed a broken jaw) while I made a quick exit to get to the international at the Arms Park.

'A year later, Mervyn Davies took his place in the Wales team as they lined up at Murrayfield – a meteoric rise up the ladder! Of course a lot of this was

107

due to the impression he had made at London Welsh where he played alongside John Taylor and Tony Gray. His progress was quite spectacular. The club philosophy, supported by the captain, John Dawes, was a strategy of all-out attack and this gave Davies the perfect opportunity to display his skills

'The next time we met we were on opposing sides. The occasion was the match at St Helen's on October 28, 1972. By now the All Whites committee had realised the error of their ways and Merv was a fully-fledged Swansea player. The game was fast, free-flowing and the tries just came and came. Unfortunately for the Tigers, the All Whites were just too good for us on the day and we lost by 33 points to 25. At the end of the match, Wilfred Wooller, who was reporting for *The Sunday Telegraph*, took the unprecedented step of coming into the respective dressing rooms to congratulate both teams for giving the crowd such an entertaining contest.

'Thirty years on, we were reacquainted when he was the guest speaker at the Walkers Stadium, Leicester. The legendary Dean Richards had been summarily dismissed by the Tigers management and Dean's numerous followers organised a farewell dinner for him. Dean was asked to pick his guest of honour and he had no hesitation in choosing Merv the Swerve who was Dean's boyhood hero. The Welsh No. 8 graced the occasion in Leicester with a superb speech about his playing days, paying due tribute to the Tigers icon. They were contrasting No. 8 forwards in style, but arguably the best ever in their position for their respective countries.'

At the start of the 1970s, another ex-Brynaman product found himself influenced by the giant No. 8. Elis Wyn Williams was a P.E. teacher at Willesden High School in North London, where some of his pupils included the future cricketers Phil de Freitas and Chris Lewis, and the footballers Luther Blissett and Dave Bessant. Elis started his career in the 2nd and 3rd XVs at London Welsh, but one Thursday evening after the weekly training session, he almost collapsed when he saw his name on the 1st XV team sheet. 'Like most players I was confident in my own abilities, but when I realised who I would be playing with, I almost fainted,' he recalls. The team to face Neath is well worth recalling : J.P.R. Williams, Gerald Davies, Keith Hughes, John Dawes, Jim Shanklin, Bob Phillips, Elis Wyn Williams, Ian Jones, Tony Baker, Trevor Davies, Mike Roberts, Geoff Evans, Tony Gray, Mervyn Davies and John Taylor.

As the team congregated at Paddington station for the journey to Neath, Elis says he had to pinch himself such was his excitement. As the 125 hurtled along the tracks, a stream of supporters armed with their autograph books were in constant attendance and high on everyone's list was Merv.

Mervyn Davies was not the archetypal rugby forward – indeed he would not have looked out of place alongside Clint Eastwood in a spaghetti western. Tall and gangly with his trademark moustache, he appeared awkward and cumbersome off the field, but once he stepped onto the pitch he was transformed into an all-action hero, a natural leader who added gravitas to any team with which he was involved.

Following the British Lions tour of New Zealand in 1971, he returned with a reputation of being one of the best No. 8s in the world. His total domination of the line-out, ruck and scrum made him a potent attacking force when that was deemed necessary, but he was also rock solid in defence. An intelligent player, Merv was acutely aware of his limitations – he was not a natural runner with the ball in hand in the same way as Zinzan Brooke, Andy Ripley or Ken Goodall, but he was always ready to learn, to take advice from the coaches of the day.

'You don't defend back there!' – he never forgot Ray Williams's words of wisdom as he retreated to the opposite corner flag from a scrummage – 'You defend in front of you!' David Smith and Gareth Williams in *Fields of Praise* pay him the ultimate accolade – 'Davies plugged holes before any were drilled. His tackling in the open field was conclusive and in the last two seasons of his international rugby career, there was no doubt that he was amongst the greatest back-row forwards of all time.'

When he fell to the ground unconscious on Sunday, March 28, 1976, in a WRU cup semi-final, he was the most-capped Welsh forward ever, with 38 international appearances. He suffered a brain haemorrhage which ended his playing career and almost his life. Remarkably, Swansea on that day scaled a rugby Everest, withstood the loss of Mervyn and prop Alan Lewis and went on to beat a strong Pontypool outfit by 22-14, with elusive wing three-quarter Royston Woodward crossing for three excellent tries. The Brynaman connection continued to the very end of Davies's playing career – outside half John Evans came on as a replacement in Swansea's back row and provided the scoring pass for Woodward's final effort. John Rees kicked the goal – all three born and bred in Brynaman!

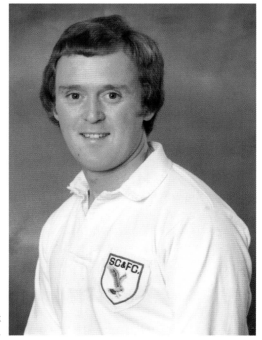

Royston Woodward, hat-trick
hero in Merv's last game.

34
David Richards

David Richards often lulled the opposition into a
false sense of security.

February 2, 1935 – a date that was etched on my grandfather John Bevan's memory until his dying day. He and a group of friends were seated in the front row of the old North Stand at Cardiff Arms Park looking forward to the encounter between Wales and Scotland. Some six minutes into the game the Welsh outside half, Cliff Jones, ghosted through the Scottish defence, initially running menacingly across field before racing some forty metres for a truly spectacular try. In anticipation of what was about to take place, the front row of the stand rose as one and, my grandfather, overcome by the excitement of the moment, hurled his newly acquired Saville Row garment into the air. That was the last time he saw his hat!

Followers of the game of rugby football from Hawick to Hamilton are familiar with the 'outside-half factory' that exists in the Welsh valleys. Most of these fans would argue that this factory came into being in the early 1950s and subsequently produced such household names as Cliff Morgan, David Watkins, Barry John, Phil Bennett, Jonathan Davies and, latterly, James Hook. For the older generation this concept was anathema as the production line, as far as they were concerned, had started much earlier. In fact, they felt that they had borne witness to the prototype on which all others were modelled. Cliff Jones, a son of the Rhondda valleys, graced the rugby fields of Wales during the 1930s and whilst still a pupil at Porth County School, his skills were evident for all to see.

David Richards from Cwmgwrach in the Neath valley started life as an outside half, and Ron Trimnell at Neath Grammar School soon recognised an individual with all the attributes required to make an outstanding rugby player. Although he was physically slight, he was very fleet of foot, ran directly and penetratively and was blessed with a devastating sidestep that could deceive any opponent. Trimnell focussed on getting the young outside half to run, thus creating space for his centres – a basic philosophy of the game. Given that David had such innate talent, this made the coach's work relatively easy.

David's rugby education continued at Cardiff College of Education under the watchful eye of Leighton Davies and Roy Bish. The college's philosophy was music to the ears of the young outside half; the aim was to run from everywhere and keep the ball away from the opposition's big forwards. There was an emphasis on skill development and within a few months the frail No. 10 also matured mentally thanks to the promptings of his enthusiastic coaches.

In September 1976, having been appointed P.E. master at Cefn Hengoed School, the young outside half returned to the All Whites that he had represented as a young schoolboy in 1972. The coach, Stan Addicott, possessed the same ideals as Trimnell, Bish and Davies and encouraged Richards to play in midfield, as the talented Malcolm Dacey was a blossoming talent at outside half. The position was to his liking and it was as a centre three-quarter that he won the first of his seventeen caps for Wales, against France in Paris in 1979, and subsequently toured with the British Lions to South Africa in 1980. Within a year, the young man from the Neath valley had moved into the world of high finance, influenced by Lewis Dick's dashing suits and flashy cars.

If there was a spirit of adventure in David's make-up, it could also be said that he possessed stacks of determination laced with stubborness. David was a skilful and silky centre three-quarter who became a Boy's Own hero at St Helen's. He varied his angles of running intelligently, always looking to release players in better, more threatening positions. There were many memorable days in the white shirt of Swansea – defeating Cardiff in a semi-final at Aberavon, an incredibly physical match at St Helen's against the New Zealand Maoris, defeating Newport in a Schweppes Cup final and those magical encounters against the Barbarians on Easter Monday. David Richards was a class act and an integral part of a highly successful and competitive Swansea XV in the 1970s and early 1980s.

Malcolm Davey, compact and competent.

111

35
Mike's Mighty Blow

Mike Llewellyn spent most of his childhood on the meticulously cut outfield at Waverley Park, Clydach, where his grandfather Oliver Williams, a knowledgeable and competent cricketer, was groundsman. He often travelled the five miles down the Swansea valley to watch his boyhood heroes perform and eventually realised his dream – playing for Glamorgan and playing at St Helen's. His finest hour was at Lord's in 1977, representing Glamorgan in the Gillette Cup Final against Middlesex. The Welsh county lost the match by five wickets but even today, thirty years later, cricket aficionados still talk about Llewellyn's innings of 62 and, in particular, one gigantic six.

The following is a transcript of John Arlott's commentary when Mike Llewellyn, for a brief moment, brought a degree of animation and certain panic to the rows of stuffed shirts sitting in the MCC enclosure in front of the pavilion.

One hundred and fifty three for five and Llewellyn really looking for runs and Glamorgan need them now and need them quickly. And they're not going to hit them hard, I would imagine, off Daniel. They've got to try to get after the slower or medium-pace bowlers. Emburey comes in and bowls. And that's tucked away by Eifion Jones down to long leg, a single only and that's really what they want, anything that will give Llewellyn the bowling. He's not a consistent player, he's rather an erratic one, but when he's going he does hit the ball very hard indeed.

Emburey goes round the wicket to the left-handed Llewellyn who goes down (*Arlott raises his voice*) and hits him sky high (*shouts from crowd picked up by the effects microphone*) – and that's six into the front of the pavilion (*sound of ball hitting the roof*). No, on top of the commentary box. (*Laughter and commotion in background.*) And that's a very, very big hit indeed. (*Applause.*) Now, that was a prodigious blow and that was as high as the roof of the pavilion and only fifteen yards short and we've made signs of surrender *(laughter)* asking not to be bombarded, but that was a mighty stroke. Albert Trott once hit one over the top of this pavilion and Frank Mann, I believe, landed on the roof – but that only wanted another ten yards carry and it would have cleared it. As Fred Trueman got up, I thought he was going to try to catch it. (*Laugh.*) I now realise, he was taking cover.

Eifion Jones, accomplished wicketkeeper, who kept Mike Llewellyn company at Lord's in 1977!

36

St Helen's to the Core

Mike Ruddock – a man of Gwent but an individual who found solace and satisfaction at St Helen's, both as a player and as a coach. David Farmer in *The Life and Times of Swansea RFC* comments, 'Whilst he hailed from the eastern valleys of the Principality, having played for the "Whites", and having come to love the club, he was a *de facto* Swansea-ite, at least as far as rugby was concerned.' And let's be honest and candid about this – but for an industrial accident, he would have represented Wales and quite possibly the British Lions at wing-forward; his destructive qualities added to his creative flair made him a hero for the All Whites, and his return as coach for the 1991/92 season proved an inspired and popular choice, earning the approval of both players and supporters. As a player, Mike Ruddock had a real presence at blind-side wing-forward; his physical attributes combined with his bravery, perseverance and vision made him a force to be reckoned with.

Prior to his return to St Helen's he served an apprenticeship with his home-town club, Blaina, and that decision was vitally important in his development as a rugby coach. One doesn't become an Alex Ferguson or a Carwyn James overnight! Unfortunately, in coaching parlance (especially in Wales) many think that the transition from a top player to a master coach is a natural one, that success achieved as a player automatically translates into coaching excellence. The two worlds are poles apart. For example – how good a communicator is the individual concerned? How tactically astute is the coach? How will he react when the team underperforms?

Mike Ruddock's term of office at Blaina RFC resulted in many trials and tribulations, successes and failures. The beauty of taking the reins at a relatively small club is that

Mike Ruddock, former St Helen's favourite, holds the Six Nations trophy aloft in 2005.

one can make mistakes without having to justify them to reporters or irate supporters. He eventually returned to St Helen's as Director of Rugby with a determination to make the club competitive, ambitious and successful. He did just that. His philosophy encompassed a fifteen-man game, but with a capability to adopt a totally different pattern of play if needs dictated. Mike Ruddock's other great trait was the ability to front-up if the pressure was on and this soon became evident in the make-up of his players.

A good coach must be a articulate and authoritative and his former players at St Helen's all testify to his fairness, all-round knowledge of the game and total commitment. When he briefly left the country and took charge at Leinster, his squad at Donnybrook was equally impressed, including the multi-talented Brian O'Driscoll, who regularly cites Ruddock as a major factor in his rugby development. Many future Welsh rugby stars were nurtured and developed at St Helen's, including Robert Jones, Scott Gibbs, Garin Jenkins, Stuart Davies, Anthony Clement, Bleddyn Bowen, Richard Webster, Darren Morris and Paul Moriarty. They all hold Mike Ruddock in high esteem.

Expectations were at an all-time high on Saturday, March 19, 2005 – Mike Ruddock's Welsh international team were chasing a Grand Slam for the first time since 1978. Anyone flying over Cardiff could be forgiven for thinking that they were witnessing the carnival at Rio or Notting Hill, such was the exuberance of the people filling the streets of the capital below. Unlike other revellers, however, in their kaleidoscope of colourful costumes, just two colours were prominent here – the green of the Irish supporters and the red of the Welsh diehards.

The Irish were in town to win the Triple Crown, while Wales had their eyes on the bigger prize – a mouth-watering afternoon of rugby was in prospect. All roads led to the Millennium Stadium, and those fans without a ticket were as likely to lay their hands on one as they were to win the National Lottery.

The hype generated in the media in the days leading up to the match had only served to heighten the tension and excitement on both sides of the Irish Sea. Every morsel of information or misinformation was analysed, dissected and pored over. Injuries to key players, team selection and tactics took second place to such questions as 'Would Gavin meet up with Charlotte on the eve of the match?' It seemed as if the entire country had gone bonkers. Ironically, even the London press got caught up in the whole frenzy, the match in Cardiff taking precedence over the Calcutta Cup fixture at H.Q.!

From early morning, the M4 was clogged with coaches, mini-buses and stretch limos with routes leading to Cardiff lined with thousands of yellow daffodils which stood tall along the roadside like Terracotta soldiers. For those 30,000 or so fans who could not get into the stadium, provision had been made outside City Hall where a huge screen had been set up. This area was promptly christened 'Henson Hill'!

The scene was now set, and the party about to begin. While, for the most part, the Welsh supporters were quietly confident (and with just cause after witnessing some glittering performances from their team) there were a few who realised that there was still one more hurdle to overcome, and that this game was no pushover. There was a small degree of uncertainty at the back of some people's minds – would Mike Ruddock's team be able to withstand the pressure? Despite my own nervousness, I was reassured, when during lunch, I heard Olivier Magne (the former French wing-forward) state quite categorically that Wales would win. He had watched both teams closely over the course of the Championship and felt sure that the home team would win by fifteen points! 'Merci beaucoup, Olivier. Cognac ou espresso?'

The party atmosphere which had been building up since dawn continued throughout the day and well into the night. According to some commentators, this day would go down in the annals of Welsh sporting history as a scintillating highlight. Over the years there had been many triumphs. 1905 had been noticeable on the rugby field when Wales had seen off England, Scotland and Ireland before finishing the year with a memorable win over the All Blacks thanks to a Teddy Morgan try. 1927 saw Cardiff City lift the F.A. Cup at Wembley in front of an estimated crowd of 100,000. 1964 was the year which saw Lynn Davies bring home a Gold Medal from the Tokyo Olympics, and in 1958 Wales reached the last eight in the football World Cup.

In the intervening years, Jim Driscoll, Freddie Welsh, Jimmy Wilde, Howard Winstone, Colin Jones and Joe Calzaghe had put Wales on the map thanks to their exploits in the boxing ring and to see Colin Jackson fly over those high hurdles made one proud to be Welsh. One must also include Glamorgan cricket's domination of the 1990s when the Welsh county asserted themselves in all the major competitions.

All of these, however, seemed to pale into insignificance on that March afternoon in 2005. Perhaps it had something to do with the fact that, just two months earlier, no one believed such a prize was possible. For the current generation of rugby supporters, the term 'Grand Slam' evoked visions of Hugh Griffith, Sharon Morgan and Dewi Morris, and was something which happened with monotonous regularity in France and England – the two teams who dominated the sport in the Northern Hemisphere.

But all this was to change during the 2004/05 season. The campaign got off to a good start with a well-deserved win against England in Cardiff and those optimists among us were predicting a Grand Slam even at this early stage. They were laughed at by the majority of supporters and with good reason. Since its inception, Wales had only managed Grand Slams on eight occasions (three times before the First World War – 1908, 1909 and 1912; in 1950 and 1952 under the captaincy of John Gwilliam and then three times during the glorious 1970s with John Dawes, Mervyn Davies and Phil Bennett respectively at the helm).

There then followed a lean period in Welsh rugby history with a sole Triple Crown in 1988 and a share of the Championship in 1994. This was not a good time to be a Welsh rugby follower. Not only was the national team playing

Shane crossing for the all-important try against England in 2005.

badly, but overall the structure of the game in Wales was at an all-time low, with no overall plan in place to develop for the future.

All this was now consigned to the history books as the nation felt itself on the brink of a new era. What or who was responsible for this resurgence in the team's fortune? It had been obvious for some time that there was a core of talented players available, but that these needed someone to mould them into a winning team. As head coach, Mike Ruddock has to take much of the credit for doing just that. While it is true that he had around him some talented coaches, nevertheless in good times and bad, the proverbial buck inevitably stops with the head man.

Ruddock's philosophy centred around the mantra 'Nothing ventured, nothing gained'. While it is true that tactics, moves etc. were worked out on the training ground, once the match was underway the coach was happy to let the players express their individuality on the field of play. An example of this was seen with Martyn Williams's second try against France in Paris and when Gavin Henson set Shane Willliams off on a run against Ireland, and this from dangerously close to the Welsh try-line.

An hour before kick-off came the news that Rhys Williams had failed a fitness test and would not play. This was in itself bad enough, but when his replacement was announced, it was thought that the coach had temporarily taken leave of his senses – he had chosen Mark Taylor to play on the wing! Taylor had taken part in only three matches since November – he couldn't possibly be match fit. Furthermore, his usual position was in the centre; he wasn't fast enough to play on the wing. What could the coach be thinking of?

Well, that was it, goodbye to the Grand Slam! The day had dawned full of expectation and high hopes, but now these had collapsed like the proverbial house of cards. Even before the first whistle, the criticism of the coach had begun. But Mike Ruddock knew exactly what he was about – in Taylor, he had someone with a vast experience of international rugby, totally committed to the cause, strong both physically and mentally. It was to be an inspired decision.

Mike Ruddock is reluctant to discuss the animosity which resulted in his resigning from his post in the Valentine Day Massacre in 2006 – he declined to accept money to disclose his side of the story in a high-profile book. 'Rudyard Kipling reckoned if you look back you're in danger of falling down the stairs,' he said in a recent *The Independent on Sunday* interview. He added, 'It's important you learn from the good and the bad experiences.' His recent appointment as Director of Rugby at Worcester Warriors will see the club challenge for honours in the Guinness Premiership – Leicester, Gloucester and Wasps won't relish a visit to Sixways with the man from St Helen's in charge.

37
Fleet of Foot

Nothing is guaranteed to quicken the pulse rate more than the sight of an attractive woman sashaying along a white sandy beach, or a Lewis Hamilton tearing around a racetrack, negotiating tight chicanes, or even those interminable seconds as we wait to see if the Television Match Official has given in our favour, as happened in the 2007 World Cup Final. During the 1970s, my blood pressure would go off the scale at the sight of Franz Klammer hurtling down the slopes at the men's downhill or watching Javed Miandad at St Helen's. The way he managed to guide the ball through the covers as it thundered along the ground to the boundary was sheer magic.

Of all the exhilarating moments in a whole array of sports, there is no finer sight than that of a rugby wing three-quarter weaving through the opposing defence and then plunging gracefully over the line for a try. Such a sight has been a regular occurrence at St Helen's over the years. One only has to recall players of the calibre of Horace Phillips, Teifion Williams, David Weaver, Simon Davies and many others who have given immeasurable pleasure to the All Whites faithful.

Of late, unfortunately, this has not been the case. All too often, as spectators file out from the match, the talk is of how few opportunities the backs in general, and the wings in particular, have been given to show off their talents. The latter especially can be seen loitering near the touchline with little or no hope of getting their hands on the ball.

Mark Titley was a player who would not have relished playing in such circumstances – in fact, never one to hang around on the periphery, he was always in the thick of the action. Even when his team was defending, Titley was always on the look-out for a chance to counter-attack. His sidestepping, balanced running and safe pair of hands made his every move look as if he had been programmed by an invisible computer. This was the era before flipcharts, video analysis and the like were in control of events on the field – to a large extent, players went out with their gut instincts.

As a result, the crowds at St Helen's were treated to some scintillating rugby, so much so that even the most cynical supporters left the ground with smiles on their faces. Playing for London Welsh, Bridgend, Swansea, Wales and the Barbarians, Mark Titley was one of those players who could make things happen.

Because their playing careers coincided with a dip in the fortunes of the national team, both Mark Titley and Arthur Emyr were deprived of illustrious international careers. Like Titley, Arthur Emyr played some of his best rugby at St Helen's; in fact he still holds the Swansea record for the highest number of tries scored – a remarkable strike rate of 154 tries in 209 appearances. When

Mark Titley – consistently produced moments of brilliance for London Welsh, Bridgend, Swansea and Wales.

these two played for Wales, you could almost imagine them going down on their knees, praying for the ball to come their way. It was the time when the forwards were being constantly trounced by the opposition which meant that the backs had no hope whatsoever of displaying their talents. I despair when I hear criticisms of some players of this era – they just did not have an opportunity to shine.

Still Swansea's top try scorer – the powerful Arthur Emyr.

If Arthur Emyr had been a Toulouse, Taranaki, Toowoomba or even a Tranmere player, I venture to state that he would have been the recipient of at least thirty international caps. Arthur was an atypical wing three-quarter for this period, in that he was tall and muscular in the mould of England's Ben Cohen or the Frenchman Emile N'Tamack. Acutely aware that speed was of the essence if he was to be successful, he would spend the summer months training with the Swansea Harriers at the Morfa Stadium. His powerful frame, coupled with speed off the mark and a positive mental attitude made him an awesome sight when on the rampage.

Arthur's physical strength allowed him to shrug off a tackle leaving his opponent clutching at his shadow. His sudden change of direction would then cause mayhem amongst the ranks of the opposition defence. Once he spotted a gap, he was away, making full use of the hard surface at St Helen's and putting into practice what he'd learned at the Morfa.

One particular game involving Arthur Emyr stands out for me. The year was 1984 and the New Zealand provincial side, Auckland, were on a world tour to celebrate their centenary. As part of this global journey, a floodlit game was staged at St Helen's against Swansea. As match referee, I scanned the team sheets before kick-off so that I could familiarise myself with some of the visitors. I knew of Andy Haden and the Whetton brothers but Kirwan, Stanley, Fox, Fitzpatrick, McDowell? They meant nothing!

I was soon enlightened of these players' talents as Swansea were swept away by a far superior outfit. The fifteen-man rugby on display that night had the most diehard All Whites supporters on their feet in appreciation. The incident involving Arthur Emyr took place just before the end of the match.

The All Whites were camped close to the Auckland try-line. The home side contested a line-out giving David Richards's team an opportunity of finishing off proceedings with some aplomb and affording themselves a degree of dignity. Unfortunately, things did not go quite according to plan. Gary Whetton took the ball in the line-out, spotted a gap in front of him and set off on a charge down the field. Before anyone else had caught their breath (including the referee), Whetton had reached the Swansea 22 – hardly surprising when you consider that the Auckland second-row forward was probably one of the fastest men on the field. The noise all around the ground was deafening with the forward in full flight and the Swansea XV in hot pursuit. If Whetton had got to the try-line, it would have been one of the truly great tries witnessed on the historic field. Then, out of the blue, Arthur Emyr appeared out of the chasing pack and, at a crucial moment, he launched himself at the New Zealand giant bringing him down inches from the try-line. The crowd went mad with honours shared between Whetton and Emyr!

38

Bleddyn

It was Robert Redford who played the lead role in the film *The Natural,* but as we left the cinema, I remember thinking Bleddyn Bowen would have been a better choice! The film traces the life and career of a well-known American baseball player, but with the inevitable Hollywood additions of glamour and romance. While it was obvious that Redford had been well coached for the role, in my opinion Warner Brothers could have saved themselves several million dollars if the Welsh captain had been offered the part.

On the beat in Cwmavon.

The ladies may argue that Bleddyn did not quite have the same charisma and sex appeal that surrounded Mr Redford, but the action scenes would certainly have been more credible. As a young man, growing up in the village of Trebannws in the Swansea Valley, Bleddyn was never happier than when he had a bat, racquet or golf club in his hand, or a ball at his feet.

His talents in a variety of sports are legendary – a goal scored in a charity match at Rice Road, Betws, would have made 'Goal of the Month' on *Match of the Day* if the television cameras had been present. The half-volley from thirty yards left the goalkeeper rooted to the spot. Another occasion saw him involved in a potential match-winning batting partnership with Liam Botham at the Recreation Ground at Pontardawe. While Botham was happy to throw his bat at every ball that came his way, Bleddyn's performance was more controlled, more classical in style – his body and feet positions straight out of a coaching manual.

Again it is said by those in the know that if he had chosen to become a professional golfer, he would have succeeded at the highest level, proving wrong those who say you cannot be good at both cricket and golf. Whichever of his talents he had chosen to develop, Bleddyn would have excelled, but it is on the rugby field that he made the greatest impression. Whether playing for Swansea, South Wales Police or Wales, he was equally adept at outside half or in the centre. His ball-handling skills were exemplary, but possibly his greatest asset was that ability to deceive and totally outfox the opposition.

A favourite trait was to run towards a tight defence holding the ball in both hands. This inevitably led to a degree of uncertainty as to which direction the ball would go. Coupled with this was his mastery of the dummy – completely wrongfooting the opposition and leaving them clutching thin air. Bleddyn could also read the game well, he could react instantaneously to any given situation, thereby controlling the game more by instinct than any pre-arranged plan. Several tries resulted from his quick vision in spotting a gap in the opposing defence. Physically he wasn't a powerful man, but he possessed an accurate left foot and the length of his kicks belied his slight frame. He was the complete footballer.

Poetry in motion – Welsh captain during their 1988 Triple Crown season.

39
Robert Jones

Every sporting enthusiast has his or her list of highlights. To some, this will include that occasion when their team won a major trophy; others will note a singularly spectacular performance by an individual. In the same vein, I have friends who seem to spend most of their spare time at various concert halls being enthralled by the music of Bach and Beethoven, whilst others can be found roaming around art galleries, captivated by the works of Picasso, van Gogh or Monet. What do we all have in common? For the crowds that flock to Glyndeborne, The Tate or St Helen's, the answer is easy. The appreciation of talent in its most heightened form.

Swansea RFC has always cultivated cultured players, particularly so scrum halves, it seems. A century ago, the diminutive Dickie Owen was a giant in the position, before Haydn Tanner proved himself a veritable master in the 1930s and 1940s. Don't forget, however, that the club has also produced a string of inside halves who should have represented Wales – Roy Sutton, John Hopkins, Goronwy Morgan, Eiryn Lewis, Robert Dyer, Huw 'Spider' Davies, Rhodri Jones and Alan Williams. According to my grandfather, Sutton was the unluckiest scrum half in rugby history, deserving a dozen or more caps. Another number nine rose to prominence at St Helen's in the 1980s, one whose genius brought colour and light to some pretty dismal Saturday afternoons. This was Robert Jones from Trebannws, who would in time convince the pundits that mastery of all the skills is required for success at the highest level. By heeding advice, practicising tirelessly, appreciating all the demands of his chosen position, and by adopting a positive mental attitude, Robert scaled the loftiest heights of the game.

His father, Cliff Jones, was a great influence, having recognised that Robert, even at a young age, had talent. A cricket bat would be a natural extension of his arms; balls of all shapes and sizes would be thrown, kicked and caught at home, in the street or on the local parks. His primary school teacher, Eifion Price, used to urge everyone in Brynaman to believe that Welsh rugby's newest and brightest star was in the ascendant. But the final coat of paint that put the gloss sheen on the young scrum half's skills was added by the P.E. teacher at Cwmtawe Comprehensive School in Pontardawe. This was Geoff Davies, and he took his responsibilities seriously. His aim was to see his school team develop into one of the best in Britain, and this he achieved during one golden period. He spent hours concentrating on the individual skills of the game, as well as preparing the whole team's performance. Robert was like blotting paper in this respect, dutifully staying after school, soaking up his teacher's words of wisdom, before going on to perfect each kick, pass and run. And Geoff knew his onions; an attractive player for Bridgend, he had also studied the latest training manuals in an effort to ensure that he could help the young scrum half reach the top.

Mastered all the skills of his position – the stylish Robert Jones.

I can remember reading an absorbing article about the tennis champion Arthur Ashe. He felt frustrated in Richmond, Virginia, as the racism of the 1950s made it impossible for a black man to get to the top. Even getting to play on the civic tennis courts was difficult, whilst playing competitively was nigh on impossible. 'If you want to be accepted,' he was told, 'you must prove that you have mastered all the strokes. At present, your backhand is ineffective.' For the next six months, Ashe concentrated on his backhand, striking ball after ball, from dawn to dusk, against the brick wall near his house. Practice makes perfect, indeed. He subsequently won championships the world over, including Wimbledon, after the six months of backhand torture! And it is the identifying and remedying of such weaknesses that became Robert Jones's trademark also.

He has become a role model to scrum halves in both hemispheres, including the current Welsh incumbent, Dwayne Peel. Maybe the Trebannws boy didn't have Gareth Edwards and Robert Howley's running game; admittedly he wasn't as muscular and powerful as Terry Holmes. But he did, thanks to application and innate ability, perfect all the skills in the scrum half's armoury. His passing was of the highest standard: there was no pronounced wind-up, his feet were in optimum position to propel the ball and draw the outside half onto it. And Robert, in the heat of battle, could pass left or right, depending on the demands of the situation.

If you consider that a sprinter who runs a 100-metre race in under ten seconds is covering ten metres in less than a second as he runs, remember that on a rugby field a second is an age. And it is such precious seconds that a scrum half's slick distribution can buy, allowing the backs to create havoc in the defence.

Robert was as two-footed a kicker as he was two-handed a passer, often dictating play subtly in defence and attack. This was seen during the fifty-plus caps that he won for Wales, and at a time when his country (and forwards especially) were under intense pressure. He would have doubled that number of international appearances had he been born in Durban, Dunedin or Darwin. There is no greater praise, and the St Helen's faithful testified to this for fifteen consecutive seasons.

40

Heart-stopping Cricket –
it has to be Matthew Maynard!

Britannic Assurance County Championship
Glamorgan v. Yorkshire
August 24, 26, 27, 1985
St Helen's Swansea
Yorkshire won by 34 runs

Yorkshire	298
Glamorgan	27 – 1 dec.
Yorkshire	did not bat
Glamorgan	237

The above result, in a rain-affected match, proved a disappointing one for the home county, but turned out to be a significant one for nineteen-year-old Matthew Maynard. In his first County Championship match, after a string of impressive performances for the 2nd XI, he scored a quite remarkable maiden century. At 185-9, it seemed all over for the Welsh county but the young North Walian had other ideas. Aided by Phil North, the two added a further 34 runs, bringing Glamorgan within reach of the Yorkshire total and leaving Maynard on 84.

Phil Carrick's 34th over of the innings will forever be etched in Maynard's memory. The first delivery turned sharply and was eventually negotiated with some difficulty. The second ball was dispatched with some aplomb into the members' enclosure just below the main pavilion, and the next delivery flew high into the air. For an instant, it seemed as if this cavalier approach would undo him but the ball eventually carried beyond the rope in the same spot as Roger Davis had clung on to Garfield Sobers's effort (before falling over the boundary) in 1968. Maynard was now on 96, the partnership worth 46, of which North had contributed no runs but defended valiantly and provided the support which was essential to his explosive partner. Surely Maynard wouldn't have the nerve to attempt another six and claim a memorable century! St Helen's was subdued; all eyes were glued on the young batsman. Carrick, who had already claimed six victims on the turning wicket, decided on some minor field changes and then slowly walked in. Maynard using his feet to good effect got to the pitch of the ball and effortlessly lifted the delivery towards Brynmill. It was an incredible effort. Maynard had reached his century with three sixes

Maynard had the ability to dazzle fans
with his array of shots.

128

and St Helen's immediately rose as one to acclaim the arrival of a superstar. Two balls later, and Glamorgan's young hero was gone – a late cut ended up in Hartley's hands.

The walk up the steps that afternoon after reaching his century was one of the great moments of his cricketing career – he had been accepted and acknowledged by his own people. A few minutes after he got to the dressing room and with his pads still on, there was a knock on the door. It was Geoffrey Boycott. He just said, 'Well played lad,' and duly walked out. It was enough; it meant a lot.

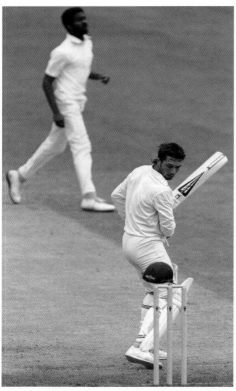

Despair for Matthew Maynard as his helmet drops on his wicket!

When Maynard is at the crease, there is never a dull moment. Those watching, especially if you are a Glamorgan supporter, are put through a roller coaster of emotions. The scene is often reminiscent of that immortalised in Bizet's *Carmen* – the infamous torero, Juan Belmonte, whose technique revolutionised bullfighting, stands erect and motionless whilst the raging bull screeches to a halt just inches away. In that instant and for the next five or six seconds, fourteen thousand people remain perfectly silent . . . the impressive stadium is eerily still, all caused, not by the sight of the stationary bull, but in awe of the main performer, the torero. For an instant, the paying customers try to visualise events of the next few seconds; expectation levels are high. This man is no ordinary torero!

There are talented individuals in many different fields who have this extraordinary ability to silence and entrance a crowd. Bryn Terfel's presence on stage before he sings a note; the anticipation of Sylvie Guillem's entry into a ballet; when Ronaldhino runs out at the Nou Camp. These are individuals whose talents defy definition; a mercurial mix of the impressive, the unexpected and, dare I say it, the superhuman. Brazilian footballers, French and Welsh rugby players, tennis stars such as Goolangong and McEnroe, all seem to have been given 'the licence to be whimsical and even eccentric'. Matthew Maynard, I would argue, deserves to be included in this category.

Matthew Maynard was born in Lancashire but then moved to Anglesey and the village of Porthaethwy (Menai Bridge) when he was seven. The sporting gene was prevalent in the family's make-up with his father, Ken, being both a professional boxer and a cricketer in the competitive semi-professional Lancashire League, whilst his mother, Pat, was a talented tennis player who represented North Wales. Both Phil Lewis and Richard Lloyd Jones influenced Matthew's development, as well as colleagues at Menai Bridge and Bangor cricket clubs. However, the real turning point of his career was an end-of-season frolic between Bangor CC and the League Chairman's XI at Marchwiel.

Matthew scored 130 and this performance impressed chairman John Bell, who made arrangements for him to travel to Kent during the following season to represent the county's 2nd XI. Several other counties became aware of the seventeen-year-old's talents and, thankfully, Glamorgan was one of his admirers. In 1985, Matthew signed a contract to play for the Welsh county, but sadly his father never saw him play as he had died a few months prior to his son's involvement.

It's celebration time once again for Matthew Maynard!

131

Maynard was a naturally gifted and instinctive batsman who had the ability to judge each ball on its merits before despatching classically (and, at times magically) to every part of the field. He had an aura about him; the bars and eating places would empty when he emerged from the bowels of the pavilion – a respectful silence would ensue as the hopes of the team and the nation rested on his shoulders.

Dennis Compton (Middlesex and England), a batsman who claimed six thousand runs for England, including seventeen centuries, was a cricketing legend. Having retired from the sport, he wrote weekly pieces for *The Sunday Express*. During the early 1990s, he composed a lengthy article about Matthew Maynard, offering advice to the England selectors. His words voiced the general opinion regarding the Glamorgan star. Compton argued that Maynard should be the first name on the selectors' list. 'This man has the ability to change the context of a game within the space of a session. Now and again he's likely to fail but just consider the occasions when he's guaranteed to fire on six cylinders and break the hearts of some of the world's best bowlers. Witnessing Maynard at the crease just takes one's breath away He must be selected on a permanent basis.' Unfortunately, no one heeded the maestro's advice.

Elfyn Pritchard in *Welsh Sporting Greats* witnessed a spectacular Maynard century at Worcester in 1997. 'The timing had a poetic rhythm about it and the sound of bat on ball and ball against boundary fence was pure music to Welsh ears and to some English ones as well. According to Tom Graveney, this was the finest innings he had ever witnessed on the New Road ground. To be present was a privilege, to witness such an innings was to see a genius at work. Maynard the supreme artist, the magician weaving his magic spell over us. Words describing the experience are an inadequate substitute for being there to see such magnificence.'

41
Swansea 21 Australia 6

November 4, 1992. 10,000 tickets sold: a sell-out. It would have been 25,000, had it not been for some unfathomable list of health-and-safety regulations. The world champions were in town, almost a year to the day after they had carried off the William Webb Ellis trophy at Twickenham.

I was teaching in Pontardawe at the time – but the TV was on in school, as part of the pupils' media studies module, naturally! Skilful camerawork and direction notwithstanding, however, nothing beats being there, either in the comparative comfort of the stand or in the rough and tumble of the terrace. The telly offers no panorama, after all.

So to capture the essence of that memorable day, as well as gain an insight into the preparations for it, I met up with Stuart Davies in the luxurious TwoCann café in SA1 on a fine September day fifteen years later. Over a hot cup of tea and chunky baguette, Stuart, with a six-year-old's enthusiasm, relived the emotions of the event, forcing me to concede that there is no experience to rival that of the sportsman who has played at the highest level. Let's face it: the referees, coaches, commentators, reporters and supporters are, ultimately, mere bystanders.

One of Swansea's greatest performances –
Stuart Davies (right) and Paul Arnold move in on Garin Jenkins.

Fifteen months before that match, Wales had been humiliated on their tour of Australia, and at the end of the 1991/92 season, Swansea coach Mike Ruddock emphasized that revenge could be exacted if the challenge of the visiting Aussies could be met with fierce single-mindedness. Which is exactly what captain Stuart Davies and his squad wanted to hear. In fact, an oath of dedication to the task was sworn by all concerned, with even the general committee, officials and sponsors rallying round. The train was on the rails!

Such was the dedication that the club's pre-season tour to Canada was not treated as a players' jolly. Trevor Cheeseman was appointed fitness coach and the team fired on all cylinders, emerging with a 100% record from the land of the beaver and the caribou, but with half an eye on the battle that lay ahead. Each member of the squad dreamt of being in the starting line-up against the famous gold jerseys come the eve of Bonfire Night in St Helen's. There was a sense of expectation, of co-operation and camaraderie on and off the field forged in North America on that tour that would stand them in good stead. They were a family.

Mid-baguette, Stuart admitted that he and Mike Ruddock had met regularly in August 1992 to discuss a mode of play that might prove effective and successful. But there were certain questions to be answered. How would the powerful Wallabies pack be subdued? The line-out was a concern: could Richard Moriarty and Paul Arnold secure enough ball for the home team? But each issue was addressed fairly and honestly, and the captain and coach explained bluntly the thinking behind certain selections.

A few weeks before the game, however, disaster struck. Ian Buckett, the muscular loose-head prop, was injured. Who would fill his boots? A distinguished former coach would come to the rescue. The hugely respected Stan Addicott was a lecturer at the university down the road and he thought highly of Chris Clark, the students' prop. Mike Ruddock watched him at work in a training session and decided to include him in the squad. Some of the press had a field day, ridiculing the All Whites front row – one (Clark) little older than a schoolboy, the other, Keith Colclough, too weak. The Wallabies manager also expressed doubts publically about the competence of the Swansea front row! But they didn't know Keith; the experts were not sufficiently expert! Keith was one of the few props in Wales who could play on both sides of the scrum, front-row 24-carat; what is more, the two props had another distinct advantage: they would be packing either side of one of the world's leading hookers, the formidable Garin Jenkins. The backs were ready for the fray also, with vice-captain Kevin Hopkins a crucial influence in midfield, and each Jack one of them thinking that victory could be theirs, as long as sufficient possession was secured.

The team was announced, but even those omitted, like Ian Davies (who had scored a try in the All Whites' 26-38 defeat at the hands of the All Blacks in 1989) and Tim Michael, though disappointed, were 100% behind the team. There was an early-morning scare: Richard Webster's knees were in tatters, but a little jog around Bonymaen seemed to convince him that he would be fit for duty.

Stuart was in his element now. The baguette had been dispatched and the animation increasing as more and more memories and emotions flooded back to him. But before describing the game, he shared one secret about the 1989 game against the All Blacks. In following captain Robert Jones out of the tunnel that day, he had slipped on the concrete outside the referee's room, before sprinting out after his captain who threw him an encouraging pass. And in front of the watching thousands, Stuart stumbled as he stretched for the ball and fell for a second time! Even before kick-off, he was muddied and bloodied!

But what of the hour and twenty minutes against the Wallabies? This is how Stuart remembers it:

Mid-morning meeting at Forte Hotel at the top of the Kingsway . . . light meal before luxury-bus journey to the ground . . . drizzly, dreary day . . . lots of the boys nervous . . . onto the pitch, butterflies fluttering . . . Aussies chose to change in the visitors' dressing-room . . . big mistake . . . no room to swing a cat in there!

A thousand thoughts as I walked around the ground . . . remember hours spent as a boy watching Dai Richards, Roger Blyth, Trevor, Merv, Geoff Wheel, Barry Clegg, Jeff Herdman . . . realise that they were coming to see us today . . . unreal, unnatural.

Preparations completed in the dressing-room . . . purposeful words intoned . . . each squad member up for it . . . news article about the 'weak front row' placed on the wall . . . motivation.

First scrum in the shadow of the stand hugely important . . . Colclough thunders in to Matt Ryan, who can't cope with the collision and pops out like a champagne cork . . . Colclough's hit inspires everybody . . . Australia on the back foot.

First ruck . . . the Whites charge like rhinos . . . golden shirts strewn about and suffering . . . I was belted, but Richard Moriarty came to the breach . . . forward he strode, fists clenched . . . the culprit froze in fear; a poignant moment as the Australians had been unnerved . . . gave everyone immense confidence.

Moriarty and Arnold unbelievable in the line-out . . . the Aussies won ball but it was scrappy . . . the All Whites back row tore through creating absolute mayhem . . . Dicky dominated the rear of the line, the back peel set up Scott Gibbs on the charge . . . Swansea had, during the opening quarter, made a statement of intent . . . the Aussies rattled.

And then, every now and then, I would shout BATH! . . . a codeword to up the tempo . . . five minutes of frenetic activity . . . ball-in-hand rugby and it worked a treat . . . Robert would tap and go, it was in-their-face rugby and, to be blunt, it worked a treat . . . the world champions were flustered and boy did we know it!

135

Scott Gibbs crossed for an early try . . . the forwards set up the platform, Robert's quick pass released the powerful centre . . . Garin swooped for a second score after an awkward tap from an Aussie line-out. Aled Williams kicked superbly . . . on the day Swansea played like world champions.

Pewter-coloured clouds were still hovering overhead . . . we couldn't see the Guildhall clock . . . Richard Webster asked 'How long left?' . . . it didn't matter . . . we knew we'd won with twenty minutes to go . . . they had been beaten in every facet of the game. It wasn't victory; it was a degree of annihilation.

Final whistle was blown . . . fantastic moment. Champagne flowing . . . missed the dressing room celebrations . . . carted away for media interviews . . . disappointed to have missed out because I wanted to soak everything in. Aussies took their defeat with dignity . . . it was a still an amateur game; we celebrated in traditional manner . . . the Brunswick was the place to be . . . players could hardly get in!

Swansea: Clement, Titley, Hopkins, Gibbs, Simon Davies, Williams, Jones, Clark, Jenkins, Colclough, Moriarty, Arnold, Reynolds, Stuart Davies (c), Webster.

42
Tony Clement

One of the most striking sights at St Helen's in the 1970s and 1980s was to see Roger Blyth timing his high-knee-lift run to perfection, taking the ball at speed, sprinting on and drawing the last man to create another classical try for his winger. Roger won six caps for his country. Had it not be for the redoubtable J.P.R. Williams, it would have been nearer thirty. Later came Mark Wyatt, a dependable fullback, a first-rate place-kicker and a clever counter-attacker.

Another who starred as fullback (but also as outside half) for the All Whites, Wales and the Lions was Tony Clement of Morriston. The rugby world probably associates him most vividly with an unforgettable contest at Billy Williams's Cabbage Patch in 1988. For the Stattos amongst you, this was the last time that Wales won at Twickenham, and it was a comfortable win largely thanks to the efforts of the Swansea fullback. Opinions had been divided over selection for the match: four outside halves had been chosen in the Welsh line-up: Jonathan Davies at No. 10, Mark Ring and Bleddyn Bowen at centre, and Clement at No. 15. The latter three would all have loved to be in Jonathan's position that day, but they would also admit that they would have played anywhere for their country.

It was a memorable afternoon for the red shirts: the forwards secured their share of ball and the talented backline used it well, scoring two excellent tries, both by Adrian Hadley, who proved too quick and powerful when put away for the line. The team would, I'm sure, however, confess that it was Tony Clement's wizadry that proved inspirational. Like Lewis Jones in the 1950s, he chose to run and counter-attack, rather than play safe. He beat one, then two, then handed on to messrs Bowen, Ring, and Davies. Not content with admiring his contribution, Clement would feature again in the move, hypnotizing his opponents with his instinctive, rather than pre-meditated play.

What, then, were his virtues? They were a veritable catalogue that included good hands, a monstrous right boot, speed off the mark, and an appetite for hard work when it came to eradicating his weaknesses. He could swerve and change pace dramatically, and it is little surprise that he spent time at the Morfa stadium with the athletics coach Tony Elgie. Speed over the first ten metres has always been key in sports like rugby, and the three-times-a-week sessions on the track were invaluable in this respect. They were opportunities not only to raise speed and confidence, but also to improve his running technique. It wasn't long before he realised that lengthening his stride would in turn allow him to escape the clutches of would-be tacklers on the pitch.

Tony has always been a keen admirer of the All Blacks. He spent a season with Wellington in the mid-1980s and was influenced by the class of players

The monstrous right boot of Tony Clement.

like Steve Pokere and John Gallagher. He worked on his skills: as one who preferred to pass off his left hand and run to the right, he practised to improve his right-hand passing and spent hours training under the watchful eyes of J.J. Williams and Phil Bennett.

He travelled the world as an international player, but St Helen's was his patch. He loved playing there alongside the local favourites, like David Richards, Aled Williams, Kevin Hopkins and the sprinter Simon Davies. Clement was amazed that Davies was never recognized by the national team: no one knew his way to the line better than the Bonymaen winger. And that observation is so typical of Tony Clement. I had hoped from our three-quarter-of-an-hour interview to learn more about him, but he was more comfortable extolling the virtues of his teammates!

43
Cotts

'That boy practising in the nets on the far side of the field. I want to see his father immediately.' The voice of the Glamorgan secretary, Wilfred Wooller, boomed out over the tannoy at St Helen's. The three thousand or so spectators around the ground, and even some of the players who were trying to relax in the lunch break, sat up and took note.

All eyes turned in the direction of the offending individual. What mischief had this unfortunate been up to was the question on everyone's lips, and none more so than Bernard Cottey when he realised that it was his son Tony who was the focus of all this attention.

Natural talent, but it was also strength of character which made Tony Cottey such a fine player.

Cottey senior hurried towards the pavilion, his heart pounding in his chest and his head filled with anxious thoughts of what the Glamorgan cricket guru was about to unleash. Conscious of the thousands of pairs of eyes following his every move, Bernard made his way up the steps to the commentary position. His worst fears were soon dispelled as Wooller strode towards him, arm outstretched and a welcoming smile spread across his face. 'I've been watching your son practising for the last fifteen minutes. It's been the highlight of the morning's play! I want him to spend the winter with Tom Cartwright at the nets at Neath. I foresee a bright future for him.'

Bernard and Tony Cottey enjoyed that father-and-son relationship that most new dads aspire to – they did everything together. Armed with a miniature-sized bat, the youngster would accompany his father to St Helen's during the summer months, and then during the winter the two could be seen kicking a football around in the back garden or urging on the Swans at the Vetch. From the time he started school as a three-year-old pupil at Crwys Primary School in Three Crosses, Tony Cottey was obsessed with sport.

While his father participated in the game taking place on the field, Tony could be seen playing happily around the boundary. A great influence on the youngster during this time was the West Indian wicketkeeper-batsman, Jeff Dujon. Not only was Jeff the professional at Swansea, but he was also a close friend of the Cotteys and delighted in coaching the youngster in the skills of batting, bowling and fielding. In Tony, he found an eager pupil, one who was willing to listen to advice and who showed great enthusiasm for the sport.

A loose delivery and Cottey flicks it effortlessly to the boundary.

When he was a little older, Tony and a group of friends signed up as junior members of the county side. A whole crowd of family and friends would make the journey to St Helen's whenever Glamorgan played there. His favourite players at that time were the Jones brothers (Alan and Eifion), Majid Khan, Tony Lewis and Malcolm Nash. He would watch intently as each plied their craft with bat or ball, trying to remember everything Tom Cartwright and Jeff Dujon had taught him as he now witnessed these put into practice.

It wasn't long before the young Cottey was selected for the Glamorgan Under 11s where he played his first ever game of cricket. At thirteen he was playing for the Swansea 1st XI and a year later he scored his first century against Gorseinon. When he was sixteen and having just completed his 'O' levels, Tony turned his back on academia and decided that he wanted to be a professional sportsman.

An offer from John Toshack to join the Swans at the Vetch was eagerly accepted, especially when he realised that the manager was willing to let him continue playing cricket over the summer months. Colin Appleton and John Bond, however, were not so accommodating. 'There's no way you're playing both games,' was their rather unfortunate dictum, and when both Tony and one Dean Saunders were eighteen years of age, they were released on free transfers from Swansea City Football Club.

This was not the disaster that it seemed at first, because soon afterwards Tony was invited to join the Glamorgan 2nd XI to play against Warwickshire at St Helen's. He scored 85 and 68 against bowlers of the calibre of Tim Munton and Brian McMillan. Wilfred Wooller's faith in his ability had been vindicated and in 1986 he was granted a full professional contract.

What was the secret of Tony Cottey's success? The following piece by the poet Nancye Sims exactly epitomises the player:

> Winners take chances.
> Like everyone else they fear failing,
> but they refuse to let fear control them.
> Winners don't give up.
> When life gets rough they hang in
> until the going gets better.
> Winners are flexible.
> They realise there is more
> than one way,
> and are willing to try
> others . . .

A fit of nerves at the crucial moment has been the downfall of many an aspiring star – and their inability to overcome them has meant that their full potential has never been realised. 'Nerves' has never entered Tony Cottey's vocabulary – he relished the big occasion. While his teammates took themselves off to a quiet room or corner to reflect, Cotts could be seen on the eve of a big match enjoying a barbecue and a few beers with friends. It was totally relaxed, but also totally prepared him for the following day's encounter.

It could be said that he was the sporting equivalent of Dr Jekyll and Mr Hyde – once he stepped onto a cricket field another side of his personality came to the fore. He was adept with both bat and ball but fielding was also a forte – defending the territory in the covers or at square leg stoutly and stylishly. He was also an inspirational figure, constantly encouraging his teammates if they had misfielded, or running over to give a pat on the back when it was deserved. I have no hesitation in stating that he would have been an outstanding county cricket captain, but that's another story.

Most sport persons admit to a rush of adrenalin just before they take to the arena – that heady mixture of excitement coupled with a degree of terror (a feeling I have only experienced once when I did a bungee jump in New Zealand!) But in Tony Cottey's case, there was a constant flow of adrenalin coursing through his veins whenever he stepped onto a cricket field. He was a bundle of energy, constantly on the move, sometimes performing acrobatic feats (which would not been out of place in a gymnasium) in his attempts to get to the ball. All of this, coupled with a big-hearted attitude, was often enough to bring about the downfall of the opposition.

When Glamorgan decided to develop Sophia Gardens as the National Cricket Centre, it came as a big blow to the cricketer from the Gower Peninsula. As a professional, however, he realised that there was a need for change and accepted the direction in which events were taking him. He, nevertheless, relished each visit to St Helen's and seemed to produce his best performances when he was playing 'at home'. In 1994 he scored 191 against Somerset (furious with himself that he did not reach a double century) and, two years later, he was again 'man of the match' against Leicestershire.

The first day's play belonged to Phil Simmons's visiting team. Taking full advantage of the prevailing conditions, the visitors amassed a total of 536 runs. Despite this impressive total, Tony Cottey's bowling figures of 4-49 were exemplary on a turning wicket. Glamorgan responded on the second and third day with 433, of which Tony scored 203 runs – a partnership of 211 with Otis Gibson (who remarkably in the 2007 season managed to take all ten wickets in an innings for Durham in a County Championship match) was a key factor in the recovery, with the West Indian contributing 97 valuable runs.

He can vividly still recall the events, and takes much pleasure in recounting his innings. 'The first half century was a bit dodgy and I wasn't sure if I'd make it to a hundred. Once I had that under my belt I relaxed – the ball kept coming onto the middle of the bat and thanks to a little help from Otis and Neil Kendrick, I managed to reach that magic figure that every batsman dreams about.'

After leaving Glamorgan, he joined Sussex where he enjoyed five successful seasons winning the County Championship in 2004 – Tony being the only Welshman to have won the title on two occasions. There are certain sportsmen whose stellar moments are played out on the international stage. One only has to think of Donald Bradman's 309 in a day at Headingley in 1930, or of Geoff Hurst's hat-trick in the 1966 World Cup final. For the majority of sportsmen, however, these moments are more low-key, but nevertheless leave an indelible mark on the individual concerned.

143

In a successful cricketing career with Glamorgan and Sussex, a career which has taken him to such diverse venues as Old Trafford, Lord's, Centurion Park, Pretoria and Queen's Park Oval, Trinidad, Tony Cottey has enjoyed many high points. However, none came close to that innings at St Helen's in Swansea in 1996 when he was playing 'at home'.

Cottey admires a deft leg glance.

44
Garin Jenkins

Fearless and competitive

Harrods, Fortnum and Mason, Heals, John Lewis, Harvey Nichols and Selfridges have to be amongst the most well-known department stores in London, if not in the western world. Selfridges of Oxford Street was established in 1909 by a certain Gordon Selfridge, a respected and influential businessman of the day.

The warrior from Ynys-y-bŵl: physically hard, mentally tough.

An interesting tale is told of a staff meeting which took place during the early days of the store. Mr Selfridge himself was in the chair and addressing his employees when the telephone rang. A young man, who had only recently joined the team, was about to answer the call when the chairman bellowed, 'If anyone wishes to speak to me, I'm not here.'

The new recruit lifted the receiver and in a polite tone of voice said, 'Good morning. How can I help you?' After a few seconds of listening intently to the caller, he replied, 'Mr Selfridge, you want to speak to Mr Selfridge. One moment please, I'll pass you on to him.' An irate Mr Selfridge took the call, and when he had finished, immediately began to take the young man to task for his gross disobedience. 'If you cannot obey orders from now on you'll be dismissed,' he barked.

Unabashed, the young man replied, 'Sir, I have been raised by my parents to be honest as well as courteous. If I can lie **for** you, then I can lie **to** you and where would that end?' A hush descended over the proceedings as everyone present nervously awaited the by-now embarrassed Chairman's reaction. Ten years on from the event, and the employee in question was elevated to the post of departmental manager.

Honesty, a healthy attitude to life and a determination to succeed. These were the qualities possessed by the young man in Selfridges, and these are the same qualities seen in the rugby player from Ynys-y-bŵl, Pontypool, King Country, Swansea and Wales – the charismatic Garin Jenkins. In a recent interview in the sporting section of *The Sunday Times*, the former Irish and British Lions hooker Keith Wood was asked to name his most respected opponent. From his extensive experience of playing all over the world, he could have chosen any number of illustrious names, but his reply was instantaneous. He chose Garin Jenkins.

Garin first made his presence felt in the maternity ward at Church Village Hospital in Pontypridd in 1966. His childhood and most of his adult life has been spent in the mining village of Ynys-y-bŵl. Apart from being well known as Garin's home, the village also boasts the fact that for three consecutive years in the 1970s it won an award as the best kept mining village in Britain!

Garin credits his parents, Eirvil and Ann Jenkins, for instilling in him those values which have stood him in good stead during his career. His roots may lie deep in the mining valleys of mid-Glamorgan, but his great grandmother hailed from Gwalchmai in Anglesey – not especially renowned for producing international rugby players. The mines have long since fallen silent but Garin enjoys reminiscing about the heydays of the 1970s when Ynys-y-bŵl was a vibrant community based around the local colliery. A particular highlight occurred in 1976 when a touring team from Argentina paid a visit to the Lady Windsor mine.

As an administrator in the colliery, Garin's father was able to arrange for his son to come along and meet the squad. As a ten-year-old, to be able to shake the hand of such well-known stars as Porta, Travaglini and Beccar Varela was a dream come true. Garin remembers them as courteous, genial individuals and when he came of age, to play against the Pumas was a special occasion, and one he looked forward to with a sense of excitement.

Dafydd Idris Edwards, Garin's teacher at Trerobert Primary School, proved an inspiring rugby coach and was also a great influence on his early years. The values laid down in the family home were duplicated in the classroom. Mr Edwards's philosophy was that if Garin and his friends wanted to play rugby, then they must also learn some folk dancing, choral singing and the like. Failure to turn up for the latter meant that they had to forfeit time on the sport's field.

From Trerobert, Garin progressed to Coed-y-Lan Secondary School in Pontypridd. This period of his life saw him develop into something of a rebel – the angst of his teenage years was very much to the fore, and he left school when he was just fifteen years of age. The following year he spent working as a farm labourer, before being taken on at Lady Windsor, where he stayed for the next four years. Latterly Garin has confessed to regretting his decision not to continue in full time education. Had he gone on to complete his 'A' Levels and then maybe a stint at college, his life would have taken a different course. But this was not to be and he admits that his pathway made him the person that he is. His early grounding held him in good stead in the long term and he is forever grateful for that.

After leaving school, Garin played for the Ynys-y-bŵl Youth XV before graduating to the senior side whom he represented with some distinction. Staff Jones, a close friend, then persuaded him to join Pontypool where Ray Prosser, one of the best forward coaches in Britain, was to play a huge part in his career. Following a conversation with Shane McIntosh, both Garin and Ceri Jones (the Pontypridd centre three-quarter) decided to accept an invitation to join King Country, a well-known New Zealand provincial team. The two hoped that a period spent playing in All Black country would prove beneficial in developing them both physically and mentally, and that they would return as wiser, more mature individuals.

The King Country coach at that time was none other than the legendary Colin Meads (a player whose name would always be included in a team of all-time greats), whose reputation as someone who did not suffer fools gladly was well known. Garin arrived in New Zealand as an unknown, but his positive attitude, strength of character, willingness to work and listen, and physical fitness soon endeared him to the former All Black. It was said that if you were able to make Colin Meads smile, you had to be an exceptional individual, and in this department Garin scored highly!

Initially the Ynys-y-bŵl terrier played for Tihoi and Taupo United rugby clubs. He was recruited into the King Country squad when the province found itself with a shortage of tight-head prop forwards. Despite never having played regularly in the position, he knew better than to decline an offer from Colin Meads, and so for the rest of the season Garin wore the coveted No. 3 shirt for King Country. Ironically, it was a game played for the province which proved to be one of the most memorable of his rugby career.

Auckland in the 1980s were a force to be reckoned with. Yet again in 1988 they were the holders of the coveted Ranfurly Shield and according to tradition were expected to select three games to defend their crown. On this occasion they nominated Wellington, Canterbury and, surprisingly, King Country. Let's put this match into its context – Auckland boasted thirteen All Blacks in their squad; they were a pretty formidable outfit with players of the calibre of Tuigamala, Kirwan, Fox, Innes, Wright, Stanley, McDowell, Fitzpatrick and Whetton on display. They had already pulverised Canterbury and Wellington and were expected to slaughter poor old King Country. Garin was again selected at tight-head prop and still remembers vividly Colin Meads's team talk uttered in a room the size of a single bedroom. In front of a capacity crowd they ran onto the field of play roused and motivated.

Ground conditions were horrendous with parts of the playing area resembling the bog just north of Tregaron. King Country adapted far better to the syrupy conditions and fired by Meads's team talk, they proved equal to an Auckland XV, the majority of whose players, just nine months earlier, had been World Cup winners. The visitors won by 28-6 but King Country were

147

labelled heroes at the final whistle. It was a moral victory for Meads's men! Garin's rugby education prospered in New Zealand. He returned to Wales as hard as nails, as tough as teak and was often to be seen exploding into the tackle area with a determination and spirit that could have disfigured brickwork.

Garin's playing career at St Helen's coincided with Mike Ruddock's period as coach. He always speaks highly of the man fron Blaina who took up coaching after his playing days were ended as a result of an industrial accident. He signed Garin after quizzing several of the Swansea pack. 'Tell me, who's the forward you least want to play against?' Ian Buckett's response was immediate, 'It's got to be that bloody hooker who plays for Pontypool!' 'He's terribly dirty,' was another comment. Garin was never dirty – he was simply a tough, streetwise front-row forward. Ruddock always got on well with his squad, and the successful period at St Helen's was down to the family atmosphere generated within the club. Put simply, everyone got on well with each other.

'I'll be picking the national team on what I see.' The words of Graham Henry addressing some eighty Welsh players who had worked tirelessly in two trial matches in an attempt to impress the new coach. He had indeed stated categorically that he would only select players on the evidence produced

Garin Jenkins – a vital try against Australia at St Helen's in 1992.

before his very eyes. However, when the squad was announced, the players immediately realised that several individuals had been pencilled in who hadn't featured in the trial matches. And others, who had, left out. Garin often relives the occasion. 'I took a long deep breath, looked Graham in the eye and without a second thought gave him a piece of my mind.'

The guru from New Zealand could have chosen to ignore Garin, omit him from the team as redress for his rudeness. In fact, to this day, the former Swansea hooker is convinced that a home-bred coach would have done just that, but Graham Henry was nothing if not astute. In his travels around the clubs watching the premier players perform, the coach had come to recognise that a player with Garin's qualities was exactly what the national team required. His faith in the Swansea No. 2 was vindicated when Wales beat the Springboks at Cardiff for the first time in thirteen contests, and then went on to win ten consecutive test matches. To his credit, the coach was the first to admit that he had made a serious error of judgement in omitting Garin from the team in late 1998 and early 1999.

There have been many events of note during Garin Jenkins's illustrious career, but none more significant than that which took place at the Arms Park in 1998. Swansea were playing Cardiff, and during the match the home side's wing-forward, Gwyn Jones, suffered a horrific neck injury. While he was being treated on the field, another team of paramedics was administering to Garin's father, Eirvil, who had suffered a major heart attack whilst watching the game. After spending two months at the University Hospital, his health had deteriorated noticeably and he had become somewhat confused. Despite this heartache, the family made the decision that, if chosen, Garin should tour Southern Africa with the Welsh team in the coming months. Not only was he selected but Garin was also accorded the honour of leading the team in the games against Borders in East London, and the Gauteng Falcons. Back home in Ynys-y-bŵl, the volume control on the radio was turned to maximum and tears were seen streaming down a proud father's cheeks as he absorbed the significance of what his son had achieved.

Garin's career, now that his playing days are over, is now developing on several fronts. He is a respected academy coach with the Ospreys, a pundit on Radio Wales (where his analysis is always straightforward and to the point) and a much sought-after after-dinner speaker, where his repartee and deprecating sense of humour make him a great favourite with members of both sexes – just ask Judith Chalmers!

The strength, resolve, determination and durability which Garin expressed on the field of play are still in evidence. Camaraderie, humour and honesty are three values which Garin puts at the very top of his list – he could have managed Selfridges!

45

Swansea RFC 22 Castres Olympique 10

Heineken European Cup 1995/96

It takes a small army of people to get a venue ready for a major sporting event and only one individual to bring the whole thing to a standstill. You may recall the scenario at Headingley in 1975 during the third test in the Ashes series against Australia. When the groundsman arrived at dawn to prepare the wicket for the day's play, he was greeeted with the words 'George Davis is innocent' sprayed over the walls of the playing arena. This in itself was bad enough, but when he realised that the aforementioned George Davis's supporters had dug holes in the pitch and poured oil over the wicket, he knew it was going to be a bad day at the office.

Another incident, which although it did not in any way disrupt the match, but was nonetheless equally spectacular, was Erica Roe's topless romp across the hallowed turf at Twickenham in 1982. It has never been officially verified but it has been suggested that it was the sight of the well-endowed Miss Roe that spurred Billy Beaumont's men onto their 15-11 victory over the visiting Australians. On June 8, 1913, a suffragette, Emily Davidson, died from her injuries after throwing herself in front of the horse, Amner, wearing the colours of George V during the Derby at Epsom. Years later, on Tuesday, December 6, 1995, the President of Castres Olympique, Pierre-Yves Revol, stormed onto the field at St Helen's in Swansea in an attempt to disrupt and call off the match – and to quote Max Boyce, 'I was there!'

There is no finer sight in rugby football than when the French throw caution to the wind and play a fast, expansive game. During the 1990s this had been the philosophy adopted at Castres and at Swansea, therefore the evening's encounter between the two sides promised some entertaining rugby. The home side was also aware that a victory by a margin of six points would ensure them a place in the competition's semi-finals.

It was a dream start for the All Whites when Castres were caught offside at the kick-off. From the resulting scrum, Robert Jones broke through the opposing defence like a whippet and with the back-row combination of Rob Appleyard, Stuart Davies and Alan Reynolds on the charge, the Castres defence was in complete disarray. They eventually regrouped but Swansea won the ball from the ruck. Before they had time to distribute across field, there was a loud shrill from the referee's whistle and Swansea were awarded a penalty. The Scottish referee, Mr Charles Muir, had spotted a French player offside in midfield and this was to be the first of many occasions when Mr Muir's whistle would interrupt what had promised to be an entertaining contest. Aled Williams coolly slotted over the first penalty which was soon to be repeated when Guy Gilbert, the Castres wing-forward was penalised following an up-and-under.

The referee's constant blowing of his whistle proved disruptive to both sides, but caused particular frustration in the French camp. Following one scrummage, Garin Jenkins, the All Whites hooker, was seen lying supine on the ground. A lecture to the innocent-looking Castres second-row forward, Jean-Francois Gourragne, for stamping resulted in another penalty, which meant that after only fifteen minutes play, Swansea were 9-0 ahead. Castres, and Mr Muir, were beginning to lose their grip on proceedings.

Instead of enjoying the rugby, I now found myself watching the referee. Although, like most of the other supporters present, I wanted the home side to win, I also felt that the Castres XV were often hard done by by some of Mr Muir's quite bizarre decisions. His body language seemed to suggest that he wasn't up to the challenge and once or twice he

Aled Williams proved himself to be a devastating runner and superb distributor.

penalised Castres unfairly and harshly for petty infringements – a word in the captain's ear would have been far more beneficial. Swansea increased their lead when Andy Moore won a line-out in the Castres 22 – the halfbacks released David Weatherley in midfield, whose long pass found Mark Taylor, who eventually released Alun Harris for the try. The All Whites were in the driving seat, leaving Castres in a state of panic and relative disorder.

And then, as if to prove a point, we had a taste of what the French club were capable of. A beautifully weighted kick from outside half Francis Rui was seized by wing Thierry Bourdet, who crossed for a simple but effective try. A second try was inevitable, but for the hapless wing three-quarter Phillipe Garriues. A quick ball from the forwards saw fullback Cyril Savy burst into the line – he broke through a hallucinated defence and released Garriues who had the try-line at his mercy. Unfortunately, or fortunately, depending on your point of view, the wing knocked the ball forward!

Garin Jenkins replied with a try for the home side, but for most of the second half the game was dominated by Castres. The forwards secured a huge

151

amount of possession, enabling the backs to attack from all points on the field and demonstrate the skills for which French three-quarters are renowned. If there was one flaw in their game, it was continuous bouts of indiscipline and Swansea capitalised on this with the help of a bemused referee.

It was now becoming a source of embarrassment, even to the most one-eyed Swansea supporter, how often Mr Muir penalised the visitors. Even when it was obvious that Swansea had transgressed, the referee's arm would shoot up into the air and award the home side the penalty!

It was all too much for Monsieur Le President. The French team had by this time realised they were in a no-win situation and took matters into their own hands. A mass brawl near the touchline resulted in the sending off of Guy Jeannard (and this just two minutes after coming on as a replacement) and this prompted Pierre-Yves Revol to storm onto the field. Waving his arms in the air, he exhorted his players to walk off, such was his disgust at what he saw as the injustice of the refereeing. Fortunately, he was restrained by touch judges Andrew Clift and Rob Dickson, and ignored by the Castres players. Swansea won the match 22-10 and progressed to the semi-final of the Heineken Cup, where they were beaten 30-3 by Toulouse.

Six policemen escorted Mr Muir to the changing rooms and were still in evidence when he walked briskly to the clubhouse half an hour later. A pane of glass was smashed in the Castres dressing room and apparently the spirit of entente cordiale was not in evidence during the after-match function. The visitors were accused of gouging, kicking, punching and spitting, whilst Castres vice-president, Patrick Thillet summed up proceedings perfectly, 'We just think he was not a good referee today.' That was an understatement, but nevertheless, if Castres had shown some semblance of self-control and discipline they could have been comfortable winners, and Pierre-Yves Revol could have been spared his moment of infamy.

46
Steve Watkin

The ultimate professional

There are many players in a range of sports who are today labelled 'professionals'. But what does the label mean? It means being paid for playing, but let's face it, its meaning is a little more all-encompassing than that! Many are paid to play a forehand, to kick a ball into the back of the net, to jump in a line-out and push in a scrum, to strike a little ball effortlessly towards a tiny hole a quarter-of-a-mile away, to paddle on a river, to punch ferociously in a ring, or bowl a short, fast delivery on a cricket pitch. But they are not necessarily professional in its truest sense. Confused? Let me try to explain.

In the 21st century, to be professional denotes an attitude, character, ability and commitment. Those players who are caught frequenting nightclubs and pubs are unlikely nowadays to hold down a place in a major team. Equally, those who womanize, burn the midnight oil and who gorge themselves are likely to see any contract they may have slipping inevitably from their grasp. A successful professional must:

An example to all youngsters; always prepared for the day's play.

   (a)   train regularly and conscientiously
   (b)   keep his private life organized and disciplined
   (c)   work on his skills, spending specific periods with a coach or peer
   (d)   conduct himself courteously off the field of play
   (e)   give 100% in practice and on match day
   (f)   conform to the team ethos and philosophy.

Steve Watkin was the embodiment of the professional athlete. During the cricket season, this subtle quick bowler gave his all for the cause; he was a cricketer by vocation and that meant preparing physically and mentally for the daily 11am-6pm challenge. He wore the Glamorgan whites with pride and conviction for almost fifteen years, and represented the England and Wales Cricket Board at international level tirelessly, proving to all and sundry that he was a cricketer of genuine calibre. In any meaningful cricketing contest, any captain worth his salt would want the Watkins of this world on his side.

153

Steve Watkin's record at St Helen's was an honourable one: 97 first-class wickets at an average of 27.09 on a pitch that has traditionally favoured spinners since W.G. Grace himself strode to the wicket at the end of the nineteenth century. One match, however, remains very fresh in the memory, a three-day championship match against Northamptonshire at the end of May 1989. The vistors fielded a host of internationals, amongst them Geoff Cook, Larkin's, Bailey, Lamb, Capel, one-time Glamorgan favourite Greg Thomas, Nick Cook and Curtly Ambrose. This was the lanky Caribbean fast bowler's first game for Northants and, thanks to a catch by wicketkeeper Ripley, took Alan Butcher's wicket with his first ball. It didn't augur well for Glamorgan.

However, the Welsh county managed to score 290 in their first innings (Shastri 50, Maynard 38, Mike Cann 75 not out – and 40 extras). The pitch was, as ever, taking spin and, in reply, the vistors were struggling against Barwick and Shastri, and only reached a total of 200. Mid-morning on the last day, after valuable contributions by Morris, Cann, Maynard and Shastri, the home team's second innings was declared. Northamptonshire had now to score 305 to win.

Captain Hugh Morris had made his intentions clear in the home dressing room: Steve Watkin and Simon Dennis would be given a few cursory overs, before handing over to the wily spinners, Steve Barwick and Ravi Shastri. All were agreed that Glamorgan's only chance of victory lay with the deceptive, spinner-friendly St Helen's pitch. 21 overs later, Northants were back in the showers, preparing for a long and dismal journey back to the Midlands. Steve bowled unchanged from the Mumbles End and took 6-42. The collapse was rapid: Allan Lamb's team went from 1-4, 6-5 to 31-7, and then total humiliation, all out for 60. Steve Watkin was unplayable.

Northamptonshire : Second Innings

A.J. Lamb	c Derrick b Dennis	1
W. Larkins	c Metson b Watkin	0
R.J. Bailey	c Derrick b Watkin	0
D.J. Wild	c Metson b Watkin	0
D.J. Capel	c Metson b Watkin	1
D. Ripley	c Morris b Watkin	7
J.G. Thomas	c Maynard b Shastri	22
A.R. Roberts	c Morris b Watkin	7
C.E.L. Ambrose	st Metson b Shastri	15
N.G.B. Cook	not out	7
G. Cook	absent hurt	
Extras		0
Total	**(all out : 21 overs) 60**	

In 1994, and in the company of Edward Bevan, the BBC cricket correspondent in Wales, I went out to Trinidad, hoping to see Steve and

Mr Dependable. A meticulous bowling machine.

Matthew Maynard representing Wales and England against West Indies in the third test. Neither was chosen. But the week provided plenty of memories. Yes, Mike Atherton's team was bowled out for 46 in their second innings, with the whirlwind Curtly Ambrose taking 6-24. But equally memorable was crossing the Savana in Port-of-Spain at the end of the day's play and seeing hundreds and hundreds of youngsters bowling, batting and fielding, dreaming of emulating the likes of Lara, Haynes, Richardson, Chanderpaul, Ambrose and Walsh. However, one memory recurs when I hear the press and media questioning the commitment of modern players. In the day leading up to the defeat in Trinidad, with the team chosen and Steve Watkin on stand-by, the Afan valley bowler was seen at his best. He ensured that those selected received the best preparation possible by exerting himself tirelessly in the nets. He would go to bed early – just in case he was called upon at the eleventh hour. He didn't complain or bear a grudge that he wasn't in the starting XI – he just got on with it and supported the others. As he ran up to bowl, in the nets or out in the middle, he mentally repeated the same mantra:

    (i)   put the effort in
    (ii) hit the deck
    (iii) bowl it with venom.

    These days, Steve Watkin is the Cricketing Performance Director in Wales. Though some despaired at the end of the disappointing 2007 season, Steve remains more hopeful, naming the talented crop of under-15 and under-16 cricketers as ones who could brighten the gloom in the coming years, just as Maynard, Morris, Cottey, James, Dale, Hemp and Watkin did in the late 1980s. One of his most pleasant memories of his career at St Helen's was seeing the thousands pour through the gates for the NatWest Cup games, particularly at the quarter-final against Worcestershire in late July 1993. Rain had delayed play for some hours, but Glamorgan managed to reach 279, thank to the running between the wickets of James and Dale, and Maynard's 84. When Worcestershire replied, Lefebvre, Barwick and Dale took the wickets, and the visitors lost by 104 runs. It was the occasion and the result, and not Watkin's own contribution, that prompted the choice of that particular match. And it is such modesty that is at the heart of this gentle and charming man from the Afan valley.

Howzat? Another one bites the dust!

156

47
Scott Gibbs

by Trystan Bevan

When noting the achievements of any particular individual in any particular field, the protocol goes something like this. Begin with background and/or childhood influences, then comment on early events in their career. Move on to a few eye-catching occurrences before embarking on a long-winded biography of goals and successes. However, when talking about Scott Gibbs, far better to cut straight to the chase. Wembley 1999.

Picasso will always be associated with abstract art, Johnny Cash with Folsom Prison, Derek Redmond with being carried by his father across the finishing line, and Eric Cantona with hurdling advertisement boards. The common thread here, however, is that they all achieved much, much more in their chosen fields of artistic expression, but they all have a defining moment which will almost certainly stand the test of time. The same applies with Scott Gibbs.

It is almost a disservice to Scott Gibbs that he will be remembered for the try against England at Wembley in 1999. He has achieved much in both codes of rugby, playing for Wales and Great Britain in the thirteen and fifteen-man game. However, a juggled ball, three sidesteps and a single-handed salute while diving over the whitewash at Wembley Stadium, London, will almost certainly be his legacy as a player. There is almost no need to describe which try when acknowledging that moment in the annals of Welsh sport. A thousand sportswriters and commentators the length and breadth of Wales have since labelled it 'that' try, in the same way that 'that' punch by Ali floored Foreman post-rope-a-dope, and that 'that' leap by Bob Beamon broke the world long-jump record. In fact, it might be argued that this was Wales's national JFK-type moment; where everyone can remember where they were when it happened, which may be both an indication of the gravitas of Gibbs's achievement, as well as how ridiculously seriously we Welsh take our national game. It was a Celtic explosion of emotion at the spiritual sporting heart of the English – the Welsh had won the game, thereby handing the last ever Five Nations Championships to the Scottish. It surely ranks up with Woosnam winning the US Masters and Lynn Davies's Olympic Gold, as a defining moment in Welsh sport.

The irony in all this is that individuals like Robert Jones, Jonathan Davies and Scott Gibbs were all excellent players during a period of mediocrity and change in the national game. Professionalism was on the horizon, and just by comparing the body shapes and skill levels of other nations to Wales at this time, it would seem the men in red were hanging on to the amateur days with all their might. Not so Gibbs, whose own might and power were two of the qualities that made him stand apart from the rest. Who can forget his hand-off during the 1997 Lions tour in South Africa, where in one moment of explosive power he single-handedly knocked the Springbok front row, in the shape of Os du Randt, off their mythical pedestal? Many an outside centre from Stradey Park to Rodney Parade had experienced this over the years, but an international prop clumsily experiencing Newton's First Law on his home turf, thanks to a stiff arm from a Pencoed boy half his weight, was almost poetic.

Scott Gibbs : dynamic in defence, blistering in attack.

48
Swansea 37   Llanelli 10

SWALEC Cup Final 1999

A coach who suppresses natural instincts may find that he has lifted a poor player to a mediocre one but has reduced a potential genius to the rank and file.

Don Bradman, 1967.

A quote from one of the greatest cricketers of all time, one who graced the pitch at St Helen's on two occasions, in 1930 and 1934. Even when he was at the zenith of his career, Bradman was never complacent about his performances. When not actually engaged in a match, he could be seen practising in the nets, perfecting his shots, adjusting his timing, and this very often with the aid of just a piece of wood and a soft ball. This was testimony to his love of the sport and his undying commitment to the cause.

There are others in a range of sports who are equally enthusiastic, equally committed and possess that same genetic make-up that sets them apart. One can think of the likes of Pele, Maradona, Cruyff, Richards, Goolagong, Best, Federer, Tendulkar, Lara, and Giggs. They are such well-known figures that they are affectionately recognised world wide just by the use of their surnames! The question has to be asked – 'How much coaching did they receive to perform at this level?' The wise coach will mould a team utilising the strengths of its players, while at the same time giving free rein to an individual who exhibits a superlative talent. This was the philosophy adopted by Duncan Fletcher during the Ashes triumph against Australia in 2005. While careful planning and atention to detail had been a feature of the team's preparation off the field, once the matches were underway then Pietersen and Flintoff were given carte blanche to play their natural game. It was a formula which proved to be very successful with England and Wales emerging victorious.

By the same token, we have witnessed many matches at St Helen's where an individual player, by virtue of his innate ability or genetic make-up, raises his game to such a level so as to leave the spectators breathless. W.T.H. Davies, Bryan Richards, David Richards, Bleddyn Bowen, Malcolm Dacey, Anthony Clement, and Arwel Thomas form such a group – and these are just the outside halves!

If winning the Grand Slam in 2005 has taught us anything it is this. If a nation of just under three million is to compete against the best in the rugby-playing world, then it has to resort to the style of play which has been perfected in the valleys over the last century-and-a-half. The 'Welsh Way' is to

Arwel Thomas, about to mesmerize.

spread the ball wide, giving the backs every opportunity of showing what they are capable of – that burst of speed, that magical sidestep, that touch of arrogance, that moment of selfishness. This is the type of rugby that has stood us in good stead in the past and this is what needs to be fine tuned and perfected for the future. It is nigh on impossible for Welsh teams to engage in a bruising forward battle. We do not have players with the necessary physique to engage and bully the big boys up front.

This expansive, open game was seen at its best in the final of the SWALEC Cup between Swansea and Llanelli, played at Ninian Park of all places, in May 1999. (The old National Stadium had been totally demolished and the spanking new Millennium Stadium hadn't been completed.) The Scarlets were firm favourites beforehand, but once the match got under way, it became clear that this was going to be a one-sided affair. Llanelli were swept away by a five-star performance from Scott Gibbs's men. During their preparations for the encounter, the players, together with the coaching staff, had considered various tactics and options to defeat their opponents. In the end they decided, by a majority, to adopt a game plan, which if successful would completely outwit the Scarlets, and leave their supporters open-mouthed in disbelief. For this plan to work, several factors would have to be considered. Would the coach Mike Ruddock give it his blessing? Would each and every player be prepared to throw caution to the wind and play an expansive game – even if this meant counter attacking from behind their own try-line? Would the forwards be fit enough to run across the field for eighty minutes or more? It was indeed a risky strategy to adopt bearing in mind that so much was at stake.

One thing which stood the team in good stead was that playing regularly on such a hard, sandy surface at St Helen's lent itself to this type of game. From the time of the James and Bancroft brothers, the All Whites had become synonymous with fast, open rugby and the opportunity of re-engaging with the philosophy should not be ignored.

The plan worked, and Llanelli were completely outplayed. Every member of the Swansea team was a star. The ball-handling skills on display, even amongst the forwards, were awe-inspiring, and with Rhodri Jones and Arwel Thomas orchestrating every move, any threat posed by the opposition was soon nullified. Arwel finished with fifteen points and was awarded the Lloyd Lewis Memorial Award as man of the match. John Billot summed it up perfectly: 'Behind the erosive power of a superb pack, the outside half delighted with his master-class display; and that deadly dummy which shredded the defence and let in Tyrone Maulin for a try was a turning point. From then on Llanelli were adrift on the river of no return.'

Colin Charvis performed heroically. He had been initially omitted having been out for five weeks since fracturing a cheekbone against England. He was included on the morning of the match and responded with two tries, continually supporting Mark Taylor, who created havoc in the Llanelli defence. Swansea and Cardiff had spent the season playing in the Anglo-Welsh

161

competition and it had been suggested in some quarters that both teams had played too many soft games against weak English opposition. Scott Gibbs refuted the claim, stating categorically that 'our games have been far more meaningful than any games in the domestic league in Wales.' At the final whistle some admitted that he had a point, even a few Stradey diehards!

SWANSEA		LLANELLI
David WEATHERLEY	15	Byron HAYWARD
Richard REES	14	Wayne PROCTOR
Mark TAYLOR	13	Salesi FINAU
Scott GIBBS (c)	12	Nigel DAVIES
Matthew ROBINSON	11	Garan EVANS
Arwel THOMAS	10	Stephen JONES
Rhodri JONES	9	Rupert MOON
Darren MORRIS	1	Martyn MADDEN
Garin JENKINS	2	Robin McBRYDE (c)
Ben EVANS	3	John DAVIES
Tyrone MAULIN	4	Chris WYATT
Andy MOORE	5	Mike VOYLE
Paul MORIARTY	6	Hywel JENKINS
Lee JONES	8	Scott QUINNELL
Colin CHARVIS	7	Ian BOOBYER
Clive van Rensburg		Marcus Thomas
Chris Anthony		Vernon Cooper
James Griffiths		Phil Booth
Dean Thomas		Tony Copsey
Lee Davies		Aled Thomas
Andy Booth		Chris Warlow
Chris Wells		Iwan Jones

Referee : Robert Davies (Dunvant)

49

Arwel

From the day he took his first, faltering steps at the family house in Graig Road, Trebannws, Arwel Thomas was destined to become an outside half. His childhood hero was Viv Penhale, the tall, muscular No.10. Every Saturday, Arwel could be found on that patch of land sandwiched between the canal and the river, which served as the Trebannws rugby ground, watching the village team playing in the West Wales League. The highlight of the afternoon for Arwel was when, at the end of the game, Viv asked him to carry his kit bag back up the hill to the clubhouse. His reward for such an honour was a can of Coca Cola!

Arwel Thomas delighted supporters at St Helen's with his breathtaking audacity.

Arwel's dream was to follow in Viv's footsteps and also emulate those other village lads who had gone on to win international recognition – Elgan Rees, Bleddyn Bowen and Robert Jones. Every evening after school and at weekends, Arwel would be found kicking either a football or a rugby football around the back garden. Saturday mornings would see him turn out for the local soccer team and then in the afternoon he would play for Morriston Boys' Football Club.

Sunday mornings would be devoted to to the oval ball when he turned out for Pontardawe RFC and it was rugby which became his first love. However battered or bruised he was after his games on Saturday, he never failed to turn up for rugby on a Sunday morning. There would be days, however, when nothing would entice the youngster away from the television set in the corner of the family living room. These were the days when Wales played in the Five Nations and on these occasions, Arwel would be glued to the box.

At eighteen years of age, Arwel was invited to join the Welsh All Blacks at the Gnoll. The team manager at that time was Brian Thomas and having already secured the services of one player from Trebannws, namely Rhodri Jones, he was now happy to have a promising fly half to cement the halfback partnership, and within the space of a few short months, the two had indeed forged a winning combination.

Rhodri, brother of Robert Jones, possessed the kind of pass that every scrum half aims for, and which every fly half hopes to receive. The ball would

163

be fired out from the base of the scrum in one fluid movement – there was no backward step, no valuable seconds lost – the ball would be dispatched like a bullet from a gun. Of course this action was not perfected without hours of practice and, in this aspect, Rhodri had a positive effect on Arwel's development. The two would spend any spare time on the training ground perfecting their throwing and catching, Arwel often complaining of being black and blue when he had not been fully alert to the scrum half's passes!

Arwel played just the one season at the Gnoll, but during that time Neath played host to the visiting Springboks. The game developed into a brutal encounter between two physical sides, which, at times, degenerated into a brawl that would not have been out of place in a wild west saloon. Indeed at one point, one of the Neath prop forwards, the late Brian Williams, was rendered unconscious during one particular melee. But, thanks to the somewhat questionable action by Gareth Llewellyn of smothering blood over Brian's face to fool the referee, the prop was saved from being sidelined. In Arwel's words, 'If Brian can get himself knocked out – we're in big trouble!'

Once the prop had recovered, he managed to inspire his forwards on to a superb performance. The halfbacks were on the receiving end of good, quick ball and Rhodri Jones even managed to score an excellent try. Unfortunately all of this was not enough and Neath narrowly missed out on a historic victory.

At the end of the season, Arwel was enticed across the Severn Bridge by a lucrative offer from Bristol RFC (and this at a time when the game was still an amateur sport). Channel 4, who are responsible for *Big Brother*, would have enjoyed huge ratings had they installed cameras in Arwel's new house. The inmates included Martin Corry, Garath Archer, Jason Kater and Eben Rollitt. Whenever the Welshman returned from the Swansea valley, he was welcomed back to Bristol like the prodigal son, because he brought with him the fruits of his mother's, and his girlfriend Clare's, cooking – and their *cawl* especially!

Nothing else in the house, however, enjoyed any kind of attention. Dirty laundry and rugby kits were strewn all over the place – half-eaten cartons of pizzas, takeaways and pasties (delivered every Sunday courtesy of the gentleman who owned the stall at the ground) were piled high on every available surface. In short the place was a mess.

On the field things were far more organised, with Arwel and his new partner Kieran Bracken controlling play to such an extent that the team enjoyed an extremely successful season. A consquence of this was that the outside half was soon contacted by the Welsh selectors to play against Italy. It was interesting to note that Arwel was always at his best when given carte blanche on the field of play. And when one thinks of Arwel Thomas, it is almost always in conjunction with the time he spent playing expressively for the All Whites. Once again he linked up with his scrum-half partner, Rhodri Jones, and it was as a result of their partnership that Arwel came of age as a player.

His slight frame belied the talent that was to blossom at St Helen's. It was impossible to categorise Arwel Thomas: he was in layman's terms 'the genie in

164

Arwel in Welsh colours.

the bottle', and when that genie was uncorked, he became a devastating runner. He might have looked like a mortgage adviser, a Covent Garden tenor or even a brain surgeon, but he possessed that lethal streak which often enables great players to cut defences to shreds.

Arwel had the ability to influence the outcome of a game. His accurate kicking out of hand was enough to demoralise the opposition, forcing them time and again to retreat downfield. At other times his distribution made for an open, attacking spectacle. One game, amongst many in Arwel's career at St Helen's, stands out. It was the 2000 Heineken Cup encounter with Lawrence Dallaglio's London Wasps. The All Whites produced a first-rate performance, completely outplaying the visitors in every aspect of the game. Arwel's was a stellar performance, amassing a personal total of 29 points, which included three dropped goals. The teams are listed below:

Swansea: K. Morgan, S. Payne, S. Gibbs, M. Taylor, M. Robinson, A. Thomas, R. Jones, D. Morris, G. Jenkins, B. Evans, T. Maulin, A. Moore, G. Lewis, C. Charvis, H. Jenkins.

Wasps: Lewsey, Roiser, Denney, Henderson, Logan, King, Wood, Molloy, Leota, Green, Reed, Shaw, Worsley, Volley, Dallaglio.

Swansea, with Welsh internationals Arwel Thomas and Matthew Robinson quite outstanding, inflicted a Heineken Cup hammering on the visitors, who readily admitted that they were powerless to restrain a Swansea XV firing on all cylinders. Wing Robinson crossed for three first-half tries, finishing off some brilliant approach work by centres Scott Gibbs and Mark Taylor. Wasps were 31-13 in arrears at the interval and skipper Lawrence Dallaglio and director Nigel Melville were in a state of shock at the final whistle, unable to pinpoint their team's inadequacies. It was to put it bluntly, a rout and it was all engineered by a magnificent forward display that somehow managed to bully the Wasps pack into submission. This gave Arwel the opportunity to take centre stage, and, boy, did he take advantage. His line-kicking was simply outstanding, the timing as immaculate as the finest Rolex and whenever he took possession the pulse of the game changed – sometimes a half break, sometimes a miss-move to set up Kevin Morgan on the burst, and always a calming influence, which infuriated the opposition. On the day, he was simply awesome, constantly taking advantage of Rhodri's accurate delivery to set up move after move. The home spectators were hysterical – it was a performance to rival great Swansea performances of the past.

He won 20 Welsh caps, scored 173 points including 10 tries (a record for a Welsh outside half) including an individual gem at Murrayfield in 1997 when the mercurial Thomas almost forgot to ground the ball in the vast expanse of the Murrayfield in-goal area – he was halfway to Princes Street! Great memories; great player!

50

Crofty – the Complete Cricketer

Where does one begin? A consummate professional on the field, a passionate Welshman, a charismatic character with a warm, engaging personality off it. That in a nutshell is how I would decribe Robert D.B. Croft from the village of Hendy in Carmarthenshire.

From that Christmas morning when at the tender age of three years, he unwrapped a Gunn and Moore cricket bat that Father Christmas had thoughtfully left under the tree, Robert decided that when he 'grew up' he wanted to be a professional cricketer. Whereas his friends had proclaimed themselves future train drivers, firemen or policemen, Robert would not be moved – he was going to play cricket at county and test-match level! His heroes were those who played for Glamorgan and he was determined to emulate them. In fact his wish at a very young age was to see Glamorgan on a par with those fashionable clubs who commanded column inches in the London daily papers.

Robert's dad, Malcolm, was only too pleased to nurture his son's talents and ambitions, and he was an early influence in his development. The two could be seen practising strokes and perfecting bowling techniques for hours on end in the back garden of the family home. As he grew and matured, Robert's talents were shaped and honed by such respected coaches as Stuart Owen, Alan Jones and Tom Cartwright. All three had introduced generations of youngsters to the joys of cricket, and their patience and vast experience all played a part in producing players of the highest calibre. Once Robert had completed his tutelage with these three, he graduated to an apprenticeship and then a contract with Glamorgan County Cricket Club.

His mentor now was Don Shepherd, one of the most respected spin bowlers in Britain. Whilst most of his contemporaries were in a state of hibernation during the winter months, Robert would spend hours at the indoor cricket school at Neath. Don would often share the benefits of his vast experience with the youngster who was a willing and eager pupil.

Once Don decided to hang up his cricket boots, he was quickly snapped up as a pundit and broadcaster. In this new role he was still able to keep an eye on his former pupil's progress. If things weren't going too well on the field, it was not unusual to see Don leave his post in the commentary box and accompany Robert to the nets, engage in deep conversation, hoping to provide an answer to the problem in hand before tossing the ball to the enthusiastic cricketer.

If the 1950s were considered as the golden era of soccer in Wales and the 1970s the same on the rugby field, then the 1990s and the early part of the new millennium were the 'champagne and caviar' days of Glamorgan County Cricket Club. As Mary Hopkin sang, 'Those were the days my friends' and

R.D.B. Croft, charismatic and
consummate professional.

they really were days when supporters from all corners of Wales poured through the gates at Swansea, Cardiff, Neath, Ebbw Vale, Llanelli, Colwyn Bay and even Pentyrch to support the team.

The strokeplay of Morris, Maynard, James, Dale and Cottey was a joy to behold, whilst the accurate bowling of Watkin, Barwick, Lefebvre and Croft made Glamorgan a force to be reckoned with on the cricket circuit. As an all-rounder, Robert provided a contribution on two fronts. His bowling was such that the batsmen facing him could not relax for a second. He was able to deceive them into making wrong decisions and bring about their downfall. At other times, he could be seen striding purposefully to the crease, swinging his bat confidently, eager to attack the opposing bowlers. This he did with great aplomb, scoring runs easily and quickly, thus steering his team into an advantageous position. As always, he was a bundle of energy, possessing a big heart and revelling in his roots and his Welshness.

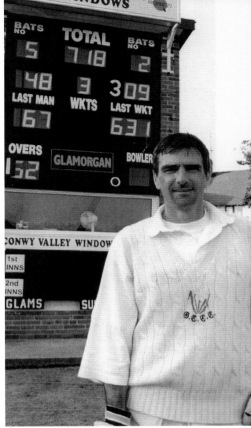

Steve James, one of Croft's distinguished contemporaries at Glamorgan.

It was during the latter part of the 1980s that a talented group of youngsters emerged to play for Glamorgan – Matthew Maynard, Adrian Dale, Steve James, Huw Morris, Steve Watkin, Anthony Cottey, Adrian Shaw and Robert Croft. To this basic core were added a few overseas players of the highest calibre. Household names such as Vivian Richards, Waqar Younis, Matthew Elliott and Mike Kasprowicz brought with them the experience and class which could only be a positive influence on the home-grown talent.

Success soon followed with the team winning the Sunday League title at Canterbury in 1993, the County Championship at Taunton in 1997 and another two one-day competitions soon after. In addition they reached the final of the Benson and Hedges Cup in 1999 and narrowly and undeservedly lost in the semi-finals of the NatWest Cup competition at Hove in 1993 and Chelmsford in 1997.

It is not always a good thing to base a sportsman's success or otherwise on statistics. This is especially true in a team game such as cricket and Robert's career at Glamorgan is a typical example of this. The team's strength during its most successful period stemmed from the ethos that everyone played for each other – there was no seeking personal glory; everything was done for the good of the team.

169

Robert played his first game for Glamorgan at the Oval in 1989. During his career to date, he has taken 1004 wickets and scored a total of 11,317 runs which includes seven centuries and 49 half centuries. Hi contribution during the one-day games is just as impressive – in 341 appearances he has scored 6,268 runs (four centuries and 31 fifties) and taken 394 wickets. Interestingly, it was also at the Oval that Robert played against Pakistan in the first of 21 Test matches. He also played in 50 one-day internationals.

I am convinced that Robert would have won many more international caps had he not made (in my opinion) the unwise decision to withdraw from the tour of India in 1992. This was made after the September 11 terrorist attacks on New York City and Washington. I remember speaking to him days before his decision became known and implored him to reconsider: 'Robert, you'll be safer in Mumbai, Delhi and Calcutta than you would be in Pontarddulais' – the latter location being the arch enemy of Hendy on the rugby and cricket fields! Sadly, he would not be moved, and I'm sure his international career suffered as a result.

A recent article in *The Observer* entitled 'Dark shadows cast by the summer game', written by former England captain Mike Brearley, and David Frith's book 'Silence of the Heart' have both alerted the public to the pressures endured by professional cricketers. This was also brought to the fore by the recent illness endured by Marcus Trescothick. For six months of the year a professional cricketer's life is spent living out of a suitcase, as he travels the length and breadth of the country for the domestic season. The press and media are in constant attention, praising one day and then delivering a barrage of criticism the next.

Another factor in Glamorgan's success during their golden period was the relationship the players developed with the media and fans. It's very rare to see players mingling with anyone once the last ball of the day has been bowled. Not so with the Glamorgan team. They welcomed the opportunity of socialising with fans and press alike – happy to discuss triumphs and weaknesses openly and honestly. None more so than Robert Croft, who relished the banter, the fun and the hype. He really was a man of the people.

Seasons 2005 and 2006 proved difficult ones for him as captain, as the team underwent a period of transformation and rebuilding. As any cook will know, without the necessary ingredients, it is impossible to create a tasty dish. The whole of Wales wishes Robert well, and hopes are high that we will see him grace the cricket fields up and down the land for several more seasons. When he does decide to call time on his playing career, a future in the media is assured. His charisma, knowledge of the game and sense of humour are a potent mix and have already assured him a position with Sky Sports.

Should Robert decide that this lifestyle is not for him – then a career as conductor of the Pontarddulais Male Choir beckons. For those of us fortunate enough to have been present at Canterbury in 1993, who could possibly forget the way he led the singing from the team balcony?

51
Kevin Morgan

by Guto Davies

'I get knocked down, but I get up again'

Kevin Andrew Morgan was born in Pontypridd on February 23, 1977, and as a pupil of the local Ysgol Gyfun Rhydfelen, came up with distinction through the ranks of Pontypridd RFC Youth.

Having been capped by his country at all youth levels, Kevin made a senior debut for his home-town club in 1995 playing on the wing, as he subsequently did on many occasions, in addition to his more familiar role of full back. Those who witnessed a frail and impish-looking youngster let loose on Sardis Road in those early days of his career, knew then that Pontypridd had nurtured a rare and precocious talent who was bound to make his mark at international level. A first senior cap for Wales soon followed in 1997, at only twenty years of age.

Kevin's rugby career, spanning the many core changes made to the structure of the game in Wales during its painful evolution to full professionalism, reflected those very changes in the succession of clubs that Kevin represented. From Ponty to Swansea (1999), then on to regional status with the Celtic Warriors (2003) before his allocation to the Newport Gwent Dragons (2004).

Kevin Morgan counter-attacks against South Africa.

Throughout all those changes, Kevin's game remained one and the same – that of an attacking genius, with an uncanny ability to hit the three-quarter line from deep with precision timing and fine angles of running. Also of a courageous defender knowing no fear, always willing to tackle well above his weight. Like others who were graduates of the same Pontypridd academy of rugby as Kevin Morgan – Neil Jenkins, Gareth Wyatt, Martyn Williams, Gethin Jenkins, Michael Owen – whichever club or region they went on to represent, they always bore the hallmark 'made in Ponty'. A rugged defiance, an awkward inability to recognise the odds stacked up against them, also a creative energy and a will to take on the world, such were the traits of the 'Valley Commandos'.

It was in the mud of Sardis Road that the genius of Kevin Morgan, from mortal clay, was created, and it was his move to Swansea, to the wide-open sandy acres of St Helen's which gave that genius the wings to fly. During his four seasons with the All Whites, Kevin was a quick-thinking, fleet-footed runner into a backline brimming with talent – the impact he made on Welsh rugby was a significant one.

A song adopted by Pontypridd supporters, as one epitomising their never-say-die attitude, was Chumbawumba's tub-thumping anthem, 'I get knocked down, but I get up again'. This could well be the theme tune to Kevin Morgan's career. His sheer bravery in the tackle resulted in a catalogue of serious injuries, most accumulated during his games in the red shirt of Wales. Time after time, Kevin was stretchered off the park, with the media predicting an untimely end to his illustrious international career. Ten major operations to knees, shoulders, ankles and other key joints of the body ensued, but each and every time, Kevin bounced back to full fitness well ahead of schedule, and always back into the Wales starting line up.

Such resilience, such courage, wired up as it was to the creativity of an attacking genius, made Kevin Morgan one of the all-time greats to grace the field of St Helen's.

52
Percy's Push

Percy Montgomery, the golden boy of South African rugby, both in the physical sense and in his status as a sporting superstar, was already one of the rugby world's most famous players when one May evening at St Helen's, he took a leap into infamy.

That night, as a casual observer of a fiery encounter between Newport and Swansea, I was one of the many stunned rugby supporters at St Helen's who witnessed an incident which far superseded the result (a Swansea win) and the fact that two other players, Mike Voyle and Ben Evans, had been red-carded. The incident occurred at the Mumbles End of the ground just after the All Whites had scored a try which had all but secured the win. Everything seemed quite innocuous, with the usual comings and goings of players retreating back behind the posts, water carriers rushing on and several small groups from the home team in animated conversation as they awaited the final whistle.

In the middle of all this, as the touch judges made their way behind the posts for the conversion, there seemed to be a discussion taking place regarding a point of law. However, during this conversation, Peter Rees the touch judge on the stand side appeared to stumble to the ground from what was later adjudged to have been a push from Montgomery. Now, as most supporters are aware, it is illegal for any player to make physical contact with a match official and, with this in mind, Nigel Owens, the match referee immediately dismissed the Newport fullback and in so doing unleashed a media storm.

Immediately the spin machine went into overdrive, with people making statements about 'watching the video evidence' and needing to 'speak with the individuals involved'. The story by this time had filtered through to the world media with tales of life bans and enormous fines an everyday entry in the sport sections of every newspaper. From Swansea to Cape Town and on to Wellington, speculation was rife. The end result was a two-year ban for Percy Montgomery. He would serve six months with the other eighteen months suspended.

Far be it for any of us present that night to pass comment on leniency or severity of bans, but the incident served a much higher purpose than simply the banning of a magnificently talented player for a period of time. It is the respect for match officials which makes rugby a great sport. It may well be a game for thugs played by gentlemen, but respect both on and off the field is a time-honoured tradition within rugby football. Swearing at referees, which occurs on a regular basis in football, is frowned upon in the fifteen-a-side game. Gamesmanship, cheating and the flouting of the rules or laws, which has become commonplace in cricket, is virtually unknown in rugby football. In cricket, immense pressure is placed on the umpires by the players, but even the

hint of dissent towards the referee in rugby leads to a ten-metre retreat, and long may it continue. The precedent of players abusing match officials was set by Neil Back when he apparently mistook referee Steve Lander for an opponent. His aggressive push led to a six-month ban.

The apparent severity of Monty's two-year ban, however, must be placed in the context of Pene Fotuaika's ten-year ban imposed by the New Zealand Rugby Football Union for striking a match official. Whatever the outcome, there can be no doubt that the significance of the incident at St Helen's in Swansea, and the ramifications on the future of rugby union as a sport of mutual respect and high standards, was enormous. The ground may have shaken when Garin Jenkins hit the turf and scored against Australia from that famous line-out steal and sprint, but the ground shook just as much when a touch judge took a tumble at St Helen's.

Percy Montgomery: World Cup winner 2007.

53
The Two Nigels!

The two Ronnies – names that are synonymous with the world of comedy. Substitute Nigel for Ronnie, and everyone connected with rugby will know that you are referring to Messrs Owens and Whitehouse, both international officials and like all referees, firm favourites at St Helen's!

How many people realise that Nigel Whitehouse, a former competitive and often explosive scrum half, played one game for the All Whites before he joined the South Wales Constabulary (where he has gone on to become a senior and much respected officer). As a member of the South Wales Police XV, he played scrum half opposite Robert Jones when the latter made his debut at St Helen's and, ironically, it was Nigel who was in charge of the match when Robert played his last game for the All Whites.

There is an element of comedy in the tale the two Nigels tell of the time they were invited to officiate at a preliminary World Cup match between Russia and Spain in Moscow in 2002. Nigel Whitehouse was to be the referee and Nigel would be his touch judge (note to Jonathan Davies at this point – they are touch judges in rugby union, not linesmen!).

As neither Nigel had visited the country of Lenin, Gorbachov, Chekov, Pasternak, Tourischeva and Solzhenitsyn previously, there was a frisson of excitement in the air – perhaps they could combine the rugby with a little bit of sightseeing. However, the weekend did not pan out according to plan.

The journey to London did not get off to a good start when the mini bus dispatched to pick up Nigel Owens turned up at Maes Lan, Bonymaen instead of Maes Lan, Pontyberem. The result was that they crossed the Severn Bridge some 90 minutes later than planned. They were up, bright and early, on Friday morning and set off to the Russian Embassy to collect their visas. Thinking it was a case of popping in and out to pick up the relevant papers, they were dismayed to find a long queue snaking halfway around the block. Two hours later, visas safely stashed away in their bags, it was a mad dash to Heathrow Airport.

International referee Nigel Whitehouse has many fond memories of St Helen's and Moscow!

They collapsed into their seats on the BA flight to Moscow with five minutes to spare. As the passengers settled down for the three-hour flight, the pilot's voice came over the tannoy – 'Owing to a technical fault, the flight will be delayed and all passengers are asked to disembark and return to the departure lounge.' To add insult to injury, the 'technical difficulty' turned out to be a faulty wiper blade. Difficult as it is to comprehend, a ten-million dollar aeroplane could not take off because of a dodgy windscreen wiper!

The restless passengers were soon reassured when it was announced that another aircraft was on its way over from Terminal One. However, a couple of hours later, the news was not so good – the flight had been cancelled! Another mad dash to the Aeroflop, sorry Aeroflot, desk in the hope that there were two seats available on the 22.30 flight to Moscow. They were in luck. Having checked in, they settled down once again to wait for their names to be called. At ten o'clock, when they realised that their names were not on the passenger list, they again presented themselves at the Aeroflot desk. It was now 23.45 and another fifteen minutes and Heathrow would close down for the night! By some quirk of fate, the flight took off at 23.55 with the two Nigels aboard. Hooray!

It turned out to be the journey from hell – they were crammed into two rear seats like sardines in a tin (or caviar eggs in a pot, as they say in Russia) – the food was awful, they couldn't sleep and were conscious of the fact that Moscow time was three hours ahead. When the two Nigels alighted in the Russian capital, the weather was freezing and when they eventually reached their hotel, there was just time for some three hours sleep before preparing for the match. Their humour was further diluted, following an hour's journey in a white van to the ground, where the match was to be played. It took Nigel (Whitehouse) less than ten seconds to decide that the match would have to be called off – the field was bone hard!

Back at the hotel, after a warming glass of vodka, the two decided to take a stroll around Red Square and wonder at the architecture of St Basil's Cathedral – no one can accuse referees of not appreciating the finer points of culture. However, after a few metres, Nigel Whitehouse slipped on the icy pavement, fell and broke a bone in his ankle. Now any seasoned traveller will know that there are two places on the planet where you do not want to experience such an accident – the Amazonian rain forest and the Russian capital.

Six hours in the Russian equivalent of Accident and Emergency, the broken bone and Nigel Whitehouse's leg was encased in plaster of Paris. Armed with a set of calipers he was transported back to the hotel again in one of the many thousand of white vans seen on the streets of Moscow. The final chapter in the drama/fiasco was played out at the airport on the following morning. Confronted by a figure who can only be described as Olga Klebb's twin sister (a figure familiar to James Bond fans), he was interrogated thus. 'When did you break your leg? Have 48 hours elapsed since the accident?' With his usual charm, Nigel confirmed that he was a friend of Glanmor Griffiths and was allowed to board the London flight. The two Ronnies would have approved!

54
The Magnificent Seven

Forever living on the edge of the law, forever risking themselves in do-or-die battles, forever bloodied and unbowed, back-row forwards are the heroic outlaws of the great cowboy film that is rugby union. And Swansea RFC can boast its share of rugged and ragged wing-forwards, desperadoes who know the clatter of smashed glass in the saloon-bar brawl and who have gunsmoke in their nostrils.

One such was Dill Johnson who hailed from Pontarddulais. He had the honour of playing in the back row for Swansea during the late 1940s and early 1950s. His strength and speed around the field was

Clem Thomas.

legendary and this, coupled with his resilience and stamina, made him a formidable opponent. His try-scoring feats were also a talking point in west Wales – his long distance effort following an interception during the Swansea v. Australia match in 1948 brought the All Whites within a hair's breadth of a magnificent victory. Shehadie, a future Mayor of Sydney, deprived them of the spoils with a last-minute try. In 1951, Johnson was at it again, crossing the line within ten minutes against the Springboks, before having the honour of captaining Swansea in a 6-6 draw against Stuart's 1953 All Blacks. He is credited with one of the fastest touchdowns on record when he scored after just eight seconds for the British Police against Devon County at Torquay.

Another outstanding player from this era was Clem Thomas. He was an inspirational open-side wing-forward, like a ghost about the field, and his running angles often created mayhem in opposition defences. His style of play is what the modern-day player aspires to, and his ability to change the tempo of a movement in an instant led to opportunities for others. Off the field he was a gentleman, but once he donned the white jersey (wearing No. 16 on his back) he metamorphosed into a hard, physical presence who constantly caused panic and alarm to outside halves. His handling skills were exemplary proving to be an effective link between forwards and backs. Clem will always be remembered for his remarkable cross kick in the Wales v. New Zealand match at Cardiff on December 19, 1953. From the touchline on the South Stand side, he was confronted by several ferocious All Blacks. In a spilt second he decided on a kick far across into the centre of the field in the hope that someone would take advantage. The ball bounced and in swooped Ken Jones 'scooping up a gift from the gods'. His try and Gwyn Rowlands's conversion secured a 13-8 victory for the Welshmen.

To be able to play in the back row, a modern-day player needs to be strong, athletic, and have a clear understanding of what is taking place around them. A boundless supply of energy is required and in addition, one also needs the patience of Job, the determination of David and the wisdom of Solomon. To be all of the above, and then to be able to stay at the very top of your game, consistently maintaining the demanding high standards, requires a certain calibre of individual. Trevor Evans possessed all the criteria listed above, and more. What made him extra special was his attitude; he couldn't bear to lose!

There are some players who draw inspiration from their captain's pre-match team talk, or the hype in the press, but Richard Webster needed no such stimulus. As soon as he put on his jersey, he was ready for action, and there would be only one satisfactory outcome as far as he was concerned – a win!

Once on the field, Webbie could be seen charging around after his opponents, making bone-crunching tackles and creating effective platforms from which his fellow players could create attacking moves. His ability to offload a telling pass just as he was about to go to ground also proved highly effective.

Colin Charvis joined Swansea in 1995 and from the very outset proved himself to be an outstanding back-row forward and crowd favourite. Physically he was a giant of a man – tall, athletically-built, possessing powerful, muscular arms. That robust physique made him a difficult adversary in all phases of the game: he was an immense presence at rucks and

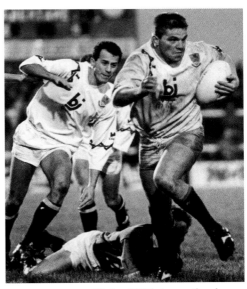

Richard Webster on the charge.

mauls. In the maul, it was a pleasure to watch the way he wrenched the ball away from opposing forwards before releasing it into the safe hands of his scrum half, be it for Swansea, Wales or the British Lions. Recently, after successful periods at Tarbes in France and at Newcastle Falcons, he returned to Wales and inspired the young Dragons to a successful campaign. His hunger and desire at the age of thirty three has been evident and his return to the Welsh set-up was richly deserved. Fifteen Colin Charvises would have possibly seen us reaching the quarter-final of the 2007 World Cup!

Outstanding photograph, outstanding second row forward – Richard Moriarty.

Physical strength, technique, endurance, stamina, resilience, bravery, commitment and a fighting never-say-die spirit were all characteristics of Geoff Wheel. These attibutes were on display wherever he played and he was a player who caused mayhem in opposing ranks. They just hated to play against him. It's the hard graft of players like the former Swansea and Wales second-row forward which deserves the plaudits and he was constantly singled out by coaches and knowledgeable rugby pundits for his all-round contribution to the forward effort. Where would those screen-hero back-rowers be without workers like Wheel?

Indeed, how often do we acknowledge the contribution put in by the forwards? After all, without possession from scrum, line, ruck or maul, the most gifted wing three-quarter is no more threatening than a Terracotta warrior. Swansea RFC has always been proud that words such as 'flair', 'finesse' and 'panache' have all been synoymous with its style of play – and that style depends on he contribution of fifteen men, not on a handful of headline heroes. There are many grafters in a chronicle of St Helen's protagonists – Mark Keyworth, Maurice Colclough, Alan Reynolds, Geoff Atherton, Morrie Evans, Trevor Cheeseman, Clive Dyer, Baden Evans, Jeff Herdman, Allan Mages, Paul Moriarty, Clive Williams and, of course, Richard Moriarty.

Richard, who captained Wales to their third-place spot in the 1987 World Cup could be described as a free spirit. He rejected convention and the commonplace. Conforming was anathema to him. On the rugby field, he was a giant – he had the strength and power to hold his own in most situations. However, it was in the line-out that he came into his own. He consistently won his own ball, soaring into the air with consummate ease, ensuring clean possession, either by catching the ball cleanly or palming accurately to his scrum half. However, he was a master in defensive lines-out, constantly harassing the opposition, and generally making their life a misery. Even when they managed to win the ball, Richard and his colleagues tore through and more often than not stole the possession.

In any western showdown, I know who I'd want on my side: St Helen's own Magnificent Seven.

55
Shane Who?

It has happened to us all at some time in our lives – a phrase or word uttered in a moment of panic, excitement or, sometimes when we are feeling mightily pleased with ourselves, then comes back to haunt us. How Ben Cohen, the Northampton, England and British Lions wing three-quarter must rue that post-match interview he gave after the Wales v. England match at the Millennium Stadium in 2001. When asked his thoughts on his opponent, the reply was a haughty 'Shane who?'

If Shane Williams was fashioned in that same mould, he would have adopted the attitude that Warren Beatty's character in the film *Bonny and Clyde* clearly relished. In the moments after they have robbed their first bank together, Warren Beatty arrogantly declares to co-star Faye Dunaway, 'I ain't good. I'm the best!' This, however, is not Shane's way. He is a quiet, modest individual, one who keeps his own counsel and accepts all the accolades heaped upon him with good grace. It is these qualities which endear him to his fellow players and press alike and make him the darling of the Ospreys faithful.

Not the biggest but has the ability to mesmerise an organised defence.

An example of his self-effacing nature was demonstrated after a particularly dour match played against the Scarlets at Stradey Park recently. As one commentator declared, 'I don't know which is worse, the weather or the quality of rugby!' In a match which tested the patience of the spectators and viewers alike, here was one moment of magic that made them feel that they had not wasted their money on a ticket.

Taking the ball on his own 22-metre line, Shane hypnotised the fast-approaching Llanelli defence with a series of sidesteps which left them rooted to the spot. The trickery continued as he sped onwards and, at the crucial moment, veered towards the open side where Andrew Bishop and Sonny Parker were supporting enthusiastically. It may have been James Hook who scored the vital try, but the eight thousand or so present rose as one to salute the genius on the wing. In the post-match interview he was asked, 'How on earth did you . . .?' Shane lay the credit firmly at the door of his fellow players. But I suspect the truth is somewhat different. I suspect Shane himself did not know how the move came about – like a tadpole which winds its way through a murky pool, it's all done by sheer instinct.

Unfortunately, not many try-scoring opportunities came the way of the Osprey wing three-quarter during the 2006/07 season. On many occasions he was forced to forage around the fringes in order to get his hands on the ball. At other times the pulse of the game changes when he appears like some spirit in the melee that is the ruck or maul and then cuts through the opposition like a rapier through fine silk. In fair weather or foul, Shane Williams is ignored at his opponent's peril.

Lionel Beauxis has Shane in a stranglehold but the winger is still determined to offload.

Why you may ask does Shane Williams merit a mention in a tale of St Helen's. The answer is simple – it was here that the Ospreys played the majority of their home matches before transferring to the Liberty Stadium. Like good wine, Shane's talents improve with age. He has a quick eye, is able to spot a gap in an instant, and this, coupled with his lightning speed off the mark, make him a tour de force. For these qualities alone, he deserves to be included amongst the all-time greats.

But it was not always so. There was a period when Shane must have felt that he was destined to play out his rugby days in the international wilderness. A point that was addressed in the BBC *Scrum V* programme and put to the then coach, Steve Hansen:

'Before we bring this evening's programme to a close, time for one more e-mail . . . and it's quite an interesting one; to be honest quite representative of the feelings expressed by many of our regular viewers. **Why is one of Wales's most talented and creative rugby players, namely Shane Williams, constantly ignored by the Welsh rugby coach?** Mr Hansen, could you please answer?'

This question was posed by Graham Thomas towards the end of July 2003, the programme broadcast on a Sunday evening after a series of warm-up matches in preparation for the Rugby World Cup in Australia. The Welsh coach, Steve Hansen, was put on the spot, and rightly so, because Williams's performances for Neath during the 2002/03 season had been quite outstanding. There was a pause, a pregnant pause before he answered. Now two seconds is a long time when you're on live television! His response was nothing short of astounding! 'Ah!' he replied, 'you must realise that we still have a few matches left to play, and Shane could well appear in one of these.'

Appear he did, crossed for two tries and left Mr Hansen with quite a predicament. Shane Williams was eventually included in the list of thirty names to represent Wales at the World Cup. I should imagine his name was the last one to appear on the team list. He had not been party to any of the fitness sessions at the summer camp, his name had not even been considered by the management team – 'Too small, the All Blacks will eat him alive' – that was the considered view.

While there was an intense and often heated debate in the media, Shane kept a low profile. When questioned, all he would say was that he was sure his time would come. He had not lost hope and was determined to prove that he could perform at the very highest level. His attitude was exemplary.

During the first month of the campaign, Shane was still in limbo. He must have felt dejected, depressed and completely despondent. He was left to care for Wales's lovespoon and even when he was included for the last match of the group matches against New Zealand, it seemed as if a bout of influenza would result in his late withdrawal.

However, when the men in red ran on to the field at the Telstra Stadium in Sydney on Sunday, November 2, Shane Williams had recovered to claim the unlikely number 14 shirt for a left wing. There is no question whatsoever that his performance in front of 80,000 spectators immortalised the quietly-spoken superstar from Glanaman in the Amman valley. What can you say when David Campese, Gerald Davies, Michael Lynagh, Philippe Sella and the likes are truly excited by an individual's performance?

When Williams had the ball in hand the pace of the game changed. Without a care in the world, he was in pursuit of perfection. His runs were ghostly, breaching defences with consummate ease. Here was a player with that peripheral vision, who never died with the ball and who was performing with a sense of danger. His footballing ability came to the fore when he finished off *that movement* . . . Jonathan Thomas, Colin Charvis, Ceri Sweeney's initial forages . . . Gareth Thomas's pass a risky one but finished with enormous flair by the enthusiastically supporting Williams. What style! What finesse! How typically Welsh!

The extravaganza continued in the quarter-final against England. The Stephen Jones try was created by the Welsh left wing three-quarter, who was by now becoming quite a star. His initial thrust caused confusion, the support from Gareth Thomas was instinctive, Shane's juggling act bringing the crowd to its feet and the final pass truly majestic.

During Wales's tour of Argentina in 2004, the winger scored three majestic tries against the Pumas at the Velez Sarsfield Stadium in Buenos Aires and the final effort was truly spectacular. I was about to interview him for BBC Radio Cymru when the great Gerald Davies suddenly appeared. He apologised for interrupting and immediately congratulated Shane on his achievement. 'Did you realise,' said the former icon, 'that you came off your left and right foot whilst scoring that final try.' Gerald was truly dumbfounded, but Shane took it all in his stride, quietly thanking one of the world's finest wing three-quarters for his comments. Shane who? That question will never, ever be asked again!

Shane Williams steps inside Jonny Wilkinson in the World Cup quarter-final, 2003.

56
Simon Jones

In a straw poll of favourite Welsh cricketers, who, I wonder, would come out on top? The results would be interesting to say the least! Starting from the day the legendary W.G. Grace led out an XI to play against the Men of Cadoxton at the Gnoll in Neath, the names could read as follows: Norman Riches, Cyril Walters, Maurice Turnbull, Johnny Clay, Dai and Emrys Davies, Wilfred Wooller, Gilbert Parkhouse, Jim Pressdee, Don Shepherd, Peter Walker, Jeff Jones, Tony Lewis, Eifion Jones, Alan Jones, Tony Cordle, Malcolm Nash, Steve Watkin, Matthew Maynard, Huw Morris, Steve James, Robert Croft, Adrian Dale and Anthony Cottey.

Maurice Turnbull.

If these are the names of the past masters, there is no question that the Welsh cricketer of the present and immediate future is that of another Jones – namely Simon, the fast bowler from Dafen, Llanelli, who played for Glamorgan until 2007. During summer 2005, there was only superstar in Wales. Whereas many in a diversity of sports promised much, but did not deliver, this young man from west Wales consistently produced performances of the highest calibre and in a team which did not always play to its full potential.

The Ashes Test Series against Australia is to cricket what the World Cup is to football and rugby, and it was Simon Jones (along with a few others) who were instrumental in winning the series for the England and Wales Cricket Board during the summer of 2005. It could be argued that in the hotly contested matches, he was the player who made the difference – taking valuable wickets at just the right moment or pinning the batsmen to the crease when it was imperative they score.

Simon Jones's talent on the cricket field derives in part from his genetic make-up. His father, Jeff, played fifteen times for England during the 1960s, taking 34 test wickets. To see Jeff hurtling towards the crease at St Helen's was a truly exhilarating experience. He was poetry in motion – the spectators' heartbeats seemed to increase with each pace as he accelerated towards the wicket. One had to feel some sympathy for the poor batsman, as the only defence he had against the red-leather missile firing towards him was the lovingly crafted piece of willow he held in his trembling hands!

There was one match during the 1968 test series in the West Indies when Jeff's batting skill also came under close scrutiny – and was not found wanting. With one over remaining, Gary Sobers's team required one wicket for

Simon Jones – superb in the 2005 Ashes series but plagued by injury subsequently.
Simon is Worcestershire-bound for 2008. We wish him well.

victory. Despite Lance Gibbs's best efforts, Jeff Jones held onto his wicket and Colin Cowdrey's team returned home victorious.

I vividly recall being on the receiving end of Jeff Jones's bowling when I opened the batting for Ammanford against Dafen in the first round of the Stuart Surridge Cup in the early 1970s. He had by this time departed from the professional scene; early retirement having been forced upon him by some serious injuries. His run-up was reduced drastically from what it was in his heyday, and his speed deteriorated as a result. Nevertheless, I don't remember seeing that first delivery. The ball was in the hands of the wicketkeeper before I had even considered moving my feet. Thank goodness the Dafen keeper was proficient or the ball would have ended up in a garden in Llangennech!

That was the father – now what of the son? Simon Jones's photograph has recently graced the pages of many a glossy magazine (something unthinkable in his father's day) and his face has become as familiar as that of Frédéric Michalak, Gavin Henson, Thierry Henry, David Ginola and Roger Federer – all now associated with modelling agencies and used to endorse a variety of products. According to my wife, Simon Jones is a 'real hunk' – therefore it was hardly surprising when he was chosen to model the latest Jaeger range for men. To quote Derek Pringle: 'Simon started the season posing nude for a women's magazine, but it was his naked ambition and determination that left an impression on the series.' His good looks, toned torso, engaging personality and success in the sporting field combine to make him a marketing executive's dream.

Jeff Jones (second from left) – the heat-seeking missile for Glamorgan and England.

Simon was born in west Wales and is a thoroughbred Welshman. It is very unusual for father and son to feature on the international cricket stage (and even more so if they play in a team to the west of Offa's Dyke). There have, to date, been only ten other instances when this has occurred.

187

For those recreational cricketers amongst us, to be asked to play for Glamorgan would be an honour, but to play international cricket at Lord's, Headingley, the MCG and the Gabba is the stuff of dreams. Both Jeff and Simon have realised this ideal – Jeff taking six wickets against Australia at the Adelaide Oval in 1966, where Simpson, Thomas, Veivers, Burge, Stackpole and Ian Chappell were all beaten by Jones's pace. The father's performance was emulated by the son during the third test at Old Trafford in 2005 when he took 6-53; Ponting, Gilchrist, Warne, Clarke, Gillespie and Lee all succumbed to the blistering pace and treachery of the Welshman's bowling.

His success is even more astounding considering the horrific injury he received when fielding at the Gabba in Brisbane during the 2003 Ashes series. He turned awkwardly while chasing a ball and suffered a knee injury which would have ended the career of many a bowler. Whilst being stretchered off the field, the catcalls and comments from a section of the crowd only hardened his resolve to return and beat the Aussies at their own game. Revenge was very sweet, therefore, come the summer of 2005. Unfortunately, more setbacks kept him on the sidelines for the greater part of the 2006 season resulting in a complete whitewash for Andrew Flintoff's men in Australia.

Simon Jones is one of those sportsmen who has consistently shown great promise but never seemed to actually live up to expectations. However, he has, of late, blossomed and matured into a force to be reckoned with on the cricket field. This success follows an intense period of determination, discipline, perseverance and sheer hard work.

High-quality fast bowlers are as rare as red squirrels, and Simon has latterly shown himself to be one of the best. He has the ability to bowl a consistently good line and length and then suddenly deceive the batsman with a ball which swings away from the bat at the last instant, ending up in the hands of the slip and gully fielders. He has also perfected the technique devised by Sarfraz Nawaz and then modified by Wasim Akram and Waqar Younis – that of making an old ball swing in towards the batsman. To do this, the ball needs to be moist and smooth on one side of the seam and dry and rough on the other. The hours that Simon spent in the nets with Waqar perfecting this technique have been repaid tenfold as witnessed in the series against Australia.

So what of the future? The Welshman has set his hopes on a full recovery from his injuries in 2007 and then he can have another crack at those Aussies. The whole of Wales will be behind him; I'm not so sure about cricket followers in Wagga Wagga!

57

9s and 10s

Whenever there is a discussion as to who was or is the best number nine or number ten, the reference is always assumed to the halfback pairing in rugby football. But this was not always so. Until the early 1960s, the number nine shirt was worn by the hooker, and the number ten was sported by the tight-head prop. Over the years, St Helen's has provided a wealth of talent in this department with many notable pairings.

To add to an already illustrious list, there is now another pair. The occasion was the cricket match between Glamorgan and Nottinghamshire played at St Helen's in June 2007. The following is the piece written by one of the South Wales Evening Post's *cricket correspondents, Robert Lloyd, who has kindly agreed to let it be included in this collection of stories.*

SOUTH WALES EVENING POST   THURSDAY, JUNE 7, 2007
St Helen's hails a new double act.
By Robert Lloyd at St Helen's

Think of all white nine and ten pairings at St Helen's and a couple of names will quickly spring to mind. Robert Jones and Aled Williams in the late 1980s or perhaps most memorably the schoolboy duo of Haydn Tanner and Willie Davies who masterminded the stunning defeat of the All Blacks way back in 1935.

Yesterday, with the oval ball nowhere to be seen, there was another local duo entering the annals of the famous old ground. In contributing 185 vital runs to Glamorgan's cause on day two of the LV County Championship match against Nottinghamshire, Robert Croft, with the No. 10 on his back, and 17-year-old James Harris, wearing No. 9, came within a whisker of the highest ninth-wicket partnership in Glamorgan history (203), also set in Swansea by Joe Hills and Johnny Clay 78 years ago. It was a memorable effort by the pair who were teammates for Pontarddulais in the South Wales Cricket Association last summer.

For Croft, his 115 was his first century for the county in three years, while for Harris a championship best of 87 not out saw him etch his name once more in the Glamorgan record books. In fact, the way he has started his county career, the Gorseinon College student may soon be getting a chapter all of his own. Last month, having just turned seventeen, Harris became the youngest Glamorgan player to reach 50 in first-class cricket and was just 13 away from becoming the youngest centurion in the 117-year history of the championship.

189

His impressive technique and temperament, especially in the face of a short pitched 'bodyline' style barrage from the 6ft 7in Charlie Shreck, is also likely to see him rapidly elevated up the county's batting order.

On 45, he took a rearing delivery from Shreck in his ribs and was left prone on the floor. But after some treatment from physio Chris Towers, he got to his feet, dusted himself down and proceeded to frustrate the second division leaders once more.

On this evidence, Harris will have to be bracketed in the category marked 'promising all-rounder' as much as 'hugely talented seam bowler' – something that watching England Under 19 coach Andy Pick would also have taken note of.

'It was disappointing not to get that final 13, but that is how it goes. Hopefully, I'll get a few more chances to do it,' said Harris. 'I have always classed myself as an all-rounder. The last couple of years my bowling has taken precedent, but hopefully I can work my way up the order. Saying that, Crofty scored a hundred coming in at number nine, so I might have to wait a bit.'

While Harris again commanded most of the headline space today – he also claimed two key wickets before the close of the second day – you cannot forget the exploits of Croft, who was playing county cricket before Harris was even born. When the former England all-rounder reached three figures with a push to the onside, there was no hiding his delight at registering his first century at a ground where he played his junior cricket.

58
Alun Wyn Jones

The eighth century was the golden era in the history of the Vikings. Those marauding hordes from Scandinavia raped and pillaged their way across Northern Europe from Russia to the Ottoman Empire and further south as far as North Africa. In Britain, Swansea and the Gower Peninsula were just two places which fell under their influence. Indeed, Swansea's name is believed to derive from the Germanic 'Sweyn's Ey' and the neighbouring Gower Peninsula has several places of Norse origin including Worm's Head – the conquering Vikings thought that the island resembled a sleeping dragon.

Today, as you travel along the coast road from St Helen's towards Mumbles, it is possible to imagine those long boats anchored in the bay – those tall, muscular warriors, long hair trailing behind them, as, shield and sword in hand, they rampaged along the foreshore.

The scene came to life one afternoon in August when the Wales and Osprey lock forward, Alun Wyn Jones, strode into Morgan's Hotel for our interview. He was the epitome of the Viking warrior – tall, athletic with finely chiselled features and long, blonde locks tumbling about his shoulders. Fortunately for us, it is on the rugby field that this 21-year-old giant does the modern-day equivalent of rampaging and pillaging!

The worlds of sport and academia are closely intermingled in the young man's genes. Alun Wyn's grandfather, Ken, and his father, Tim (a respected Swansea solicitor) have both played for the All Whites. His maternal grandmother, Ruth, hailed from Dinas Mawddwy in North Wales and was a former student of the academics and poets, Gwenallt and Sir T.H. Parry Williams. His mother, Ann, is quite an authority on the life and times of Owain Glyndŵr – another who would choose the Welsh prince as his specialist subject on *'Mastermind'* is the former Wales centre three-quarter, Ray Gravell. When the two met in the bar of the Hotel Metropole in Rome recently, we were all intrigued as to the outcome of their discussion. Grav challenged Mrs Jones to ask him anything about Glyndŵr. When he couldn't answer the first question, Ray's response was 'Ask me another question about Owain Glyndŵr!'

Alun Wyn Jones received his early education at Oystermouth Primary School. From there, he moved onto Bishop Gore Comprehensive where he won a scholarship which took him to the sixth form at Llandovery College. Mindful of the school's tradition of producing international rugby players, individuals of the calibre of Vivian Jenkins, Cliff Jones, Arthur Rees, Kingsley Jones, Aled Williams, Gwyn Jones, Peter Rogers and the Quinnells, it was a proud Jones family who saw Alun Wyn's name in gold lettering added to the board of distinguished old boys who had worn the red jersey.

During our conversation, the young man from Mumbles was full of praise

and admiration for the various coaches from Mumbles to Bonymaen, from Swansea to the Ospreys and Wales who had helped him during his career thus far. As we tucked into our coffee and biscuits, the one thing I found intriguing, and yet refreshing, about this young man was his philosophy on life.

He realises that the career of a professional sportsman can be a short one. It can be curtailed suddenly due to injury, age or to the instant appearance of a new kid on the block and, because of this, he had already made contingency plans for the future. At the moment, he is two years into a course which will allow him to finish with a law degree. The authorities at the University College of Wales, Swansea have allowed him to extend his time there from three to five years to enable him to carry out his rugby commitments. They also realise the kudos that an international sportsman on campus brings to the college. Alun's philosophy is simple, 'Success on the field is of the utmost importance, but success off it is paramount.'

Seventeen international caps within the space of seventeen months is no mean feat for any young player. The first was won in a baptism of fire against the Pumas in the Patagonian heartland of Puerto Madryn in June 2006. The supporters, a significant proportion of whom were Welsh-speaking Argentinians, were vociferous in their support of the home team, while at the same time equally appreciative of the skills displayed by the men in red. The national team seriously underperformed during the 2006/07 season but Alun Wyn Jones managed to maintain a consistently high standard of play. Without doubt, he will be a permanent fixture at lock forward for the foreseeable future.

James Hook, Aled Brew, Ian Evans and Alun Wyn Jones are four young Ospreys who have experienced extensive coverage in the press and media during the last season. While it is commonplace to shine the spotlight on the ballerinas in the back division, it is very rare to highlight those shire horses in the pack. Alun Wyn Jones is a player whose talent straddles both aspects of play – strong enough to hold his own in the contact areas of the scrum, ruck, maul and line-out, but athletic enough and fast enough to run with the ball in hand. If only we had eight A.W. Joneses in the national team, we could take on and beat any team in the world.

Having achieved one aim by playing for his country, his next ambition is to tour with the British Lions, following in the footsteps of other St Helen's luminaries such as Rowe Harding, Haydn Tanner, Clem Thomas, W.O. Williams, John Faull, Dewi Bebb, Trevor Evans, and others.

After each game he will spend hours studying the match DVDs, analysing his own performance and those of his opponents. Is there room for improvement in his own game? 'Of course,' was the immediate reply. By studying the way such players as Paul O'Connell and Justin Harrison go about their business, Alun Wyn hopes to learn some of the tricks of the trade.

Alun Wyn Jones has been described as the new John Eales – he has the making of a great captain.

'There's a bit about him,' he says of Ulster lock Harrison. 'He's an awkward customer.' His proudest moment to date is playing alongside his boyhood hero, Martyn Williams, and obviously crossing for his first international try against Argentina at the Millennium Stadium in the World Cup preparatory match.

The prospect of playing in France one day is also one that he relishes. Ironically father Tim Jones was Fabrice Landreau's agent when the Frenchman played at Bridgend and Neath – the families remain friends to this present day. It would not come as any great surprise, now that Landreau is one of the head coaches at Stade Français, to see the son playing in the pink shirt of the Parisian club.

It was a pink shirt that he wore on the day of our interview, making him look like one of those surfers in *Baywatch* – and given that he spends the occasional day sailing across Swansea Bay, I was tempted to ask if he had any Scandinavian ancestors!

59

The Five Wisden Cricketers
of the Century –
and they all played at St Helen's!

1) Sir Donald Bradman

The world's greatest ever batsman. The boy from Bowral was simply the best. Never coached, never told how to hold a bat. Practised with just a stump and a golf ball. From day to day he learnt how to pull, hook, straight drive, square cut, glance and off-drive; you name the stoke and Bradman perfected it. He accumulated 28,067 runs at an average of 95.14 . . . 37 became double hundreds . . . 5 were triples . . . one quadruple! Scored 309 in a single day for Australia against England at Headingley in 1930. In Test matches he scored 117 hundreds from 338 innings – a ratio of a century in every 2.89 innings. Averaged 56.57 during the infamous Bodyline series in 1932/33. Constantly humiliated the opposition. Lightning feet. A will to win. Immense powers of concentration. A machine in terms of run-getting.

Bradman's Test scores in England:
* – not out

1930

Trent Bridge:	8	131
Lord's:	254	1
Headingley:	334	
Old Trafford:	14	
Kennington Oval:	232	

1934

Trent Bridge:	29	25
Lord's:	36	13
Old Trafford:	30	
Headingley:	304	
Kennington Oval:	244	77

Sir Donald Bradman

1938			1948		
Trent Bridge:	51	144*	Trent Bridge:	138	0
Lord's:	18	102*	Lord's:	38	89
Old Trafford:	abandoned		Old Trafford:	7	30*
Headingley:	103	16	Headingley:	33	173*
Kennington Oval:	absent hurt		Kennington Oval:	0	

D.G. BRADMAN : Individual Career Test Record.

Tests	Innings	NO	Runs	HS	Avge	100	50
52	80	10	6996	334	99.94	29	13

That Final Test Innings :

Required just four runs to end his Test career with an average of 100. Eric Hollies fired a googly. Perfect length. Bradman stretched forward, played outside the line and was bowled between bat and pad. Dramatic end to an unbelievable reign.

Ted A'Beckett, who played with Sir Don Bradman for Australia in the 1930s, encapsulates the greatness of the batsman and the man:

He was the original smiling assassin. Because he was so small in stature, people underestimated his capacity to utterly destroy and demoralise the opposition. He enjoyed the challenge to tackle, beat and then obliterate every bowler he ever faced at every level of the game. From O'Reilly to Larwood, he delivered such fearful hidings that even those greats wished they had taken up other sports. He was the most gentlemanly, polite, ruthless and efficient sporting dominator who ever lived.

Post Script :

And he played at St Helen's. Twice. In 1930 and 1938.

1930:
First Innings:
D.G. Bradman   b Ryan   58

Second Innings:
D.G. Bradman   not out   19

1938:
D.G. Bradman   st H.G. Davies b Clay   17

196

2) Sir John (Jack) Berry Hobbs.

His nickname 'The Master' says it all but here are some facts: 61 test matches . . . a total of 61,237 runs in first-class cricket, including 197 centuries . . . 98 centuries scored when he had passed his fortieth birthday . . . Twenty centuries scored before lunch on the first day (many batsmen dream of achieving this feat just once) . . . like Don Bradman, Jack Hobbs was a natural talent who did not require the services of a coach . . . his total of 316 not out against Middlesex at Lord's was a record which stood until 1990 when Graham Gooch surpassed him, scoring 333 not out against India . . . first professional cricketer to lead England when he captained the side against Australia at Old Trafford in 1926 . . . popular figure and in 1953 the first cricketer to be knighted for his services to the game. (The above figures are even more remarkable when you realise that no cricket was played for four years during the period of the Great War).

J.B. HOBBS: Individual Career Test Record.

Tests	Innings	NO	Runs	HS	Avge	100	50
61	102	7	5410	211	56.94	15	28

Post script:

And he played at St Helen's. Twice. In 1930 and 1932.

1930:
First Innings:
J.B. Hobbs   run out   21

1934:
First Innings:
J.B. Hobbs   c Every b Jones   21

3) Sir Garfield Sobers

There is a separate chapter on the West Indian all-rounder in the book but I would like to tell an amusing anecdote relating to the day when Sobers hit those six sixes off the bowling of Malcolm Nash at St Helen's.

A substantial group of supporters had decided that during the lunch interval in the game between Glamorgan and Nottinghamshire, they would wander down the road to watch the Swans kick off the new season at the Vetch. This way they would be guaranteed a little bit of action if the cricket became defensive and uninteresting. Little did they realise that while they watched a mediocre soccer match which ended goal-less, they missed the fireworks and the history that was being played out back at St Helen's.

G.St A. SOBERS: Individual Career Test Record.

Batting:

Tests	Innings	NO	Runs	HS	Avge	100	50
93	160	21	8032	365*	57.78	26	30

Bowling :

Balls	Runs	Wkts	Avge	BB
21599	7999	235	34.03	6-73

Fielding:
109 catches.

Post script:

Played at St Helen's for the West Indies and Nottinghamshire for whom he scored 151* in 1971.

Sir Garfield Sobers – as great a bowler as he was a batsman.

4) Shane Warne

S. K. WARNE: Individual Career Test Record.

Balls	Runs	Wkts	Avge	BB
40,705	17995	708	25.41	8-91

One Day Internationals:

Balls	Runs	Wkts	Avge	BB
10,642	7,541	293	25.73	5-33

On the back pages of newspapers the world over there were tales of legbreaks and flippers. At other times, his name appeared on front pages and even on page three in a certain British tabloid – diet pills, women, a bookmaker, even more women and pictures to prove it. Shane Warne was deservedly included in that coveted list in 2000, when a hundred of the world's journalists chose their cricketers of the century. To be honest, cricket followers from Antigua to Adelaide would have included S.K. Warne in their top three let alone a top five. He has been a simply awesome test cricketer! From the moment he bamboozled Mike Gatting with that delivery which pitched outside leg stump, spun menacingly out of Gatting's reach and totally demolished his off stump, Warne became a legend in the space of five seconds. I suppose that like Frank Lloyd Wright, Leonardo da Vinci and Mozart, the youngster from Upper Ferntree Gully in Victoria, having discovered simplicity, went on to become recognised and respected the world over. Shane Keith Warne has, during the past decade, managed to revive a dying art.

Despite the fact that I consider cricket my first love, I have to confess that I had never seen Shane Warne play in the flesh. However, when I realised that he would be leading the Hampshire team at St Helen's in the summer of 2007, I realised that my wish would soon be fulfilled. After all, I wanted to be able to say to my grandchildren, 'I saw the world's greatest ever spin bowler in action at St Helen's.' We arrived at the ground just in time to see him strike a huge six into the pavilion area, eventually scoring 18 not out in an impressive Hampshire total of 283-6 in 50 overs.

Warne then led his team onto the field for the Glamorgan innings, after all he is, in the opinion of many commentators and journalists, 'the best captain Australia never had'. His lifestyle and off-the-field activities were factors which led the Australian selectors to ignore the claims of this muti-talented cricketer. Be that as it may, he had the ability to get the best out of his team-mates, encouraging them, urging them on, and sympathetic when mistakes were made. This went on continuously throughout the innings and it became evident after only a few overs which team would win the match. Warne himself bowled 8 overs and took 2-32.

Like me, the vast majority of supporters had come to see Warne and he did not disappoint. My lasting memory of him is of the blonde figure besieged by autograph hunters outside the dressing room. He must have signed his signature a hundred times or more and had his photograph taken with every child on the ground until he eventually declared, 'Are you all done? I want a shower!

Shane Warne graced St Helen's with his presence in the summer of 2007 – one of the all-time greats.

5) Sir Vivian Richards

Viv Richards would be included in any cricket aficionado's dream team. There would of course be a great deal of debate regarding the opening batsmen – would it be Hobbs, Hutton, Gavaskar, Greenidge, Haynes, Barry Richards or Hayden? Would you include Lara or Tendulkar? But there would always be a slot for the maestro from Antigua.

Sir Isaac Vivian Alexander Richards – the 'Master Blaster' who represented the Combined Islands, the Leeward Islands, Somerset, Queensland, the West Indies . . . and Glamorgan.

In the modern game, where the batsmen are so well protected that it is always impossible to identify them under their helmets, it was always refreshing to see Viv stride out onto the pitch in his trademark red West Indies cap, seemingly without a care in the world.

There were some mutterings in Wales when, at the age of 38 and with his international career at an end, Viv Richards agreed a lucrative contract with Glamorgan. From the time he first stepped onto the field as a Glamorgan player in 1990, he proved an inspirational signing. His record at the club speaks for itself :

First class career:

Batting:

M's	Innings	NO	Runs	HS	Avge	100	50
49	83	11	3382	224*	46.97	10	14

List A Matches (one day):
Batting

M's	Innings	NO	Runs	HS	Avge	100	50
61	58	10	1921	162*	40.02	3	9

Bowling

Balls	Runs	Wkts	Avge	BB
1934	1463	55	26.60	3-12

I.V.A. RICHARDS: Individual Career Test Record.

Batting:

Tests	Innings	NO	Runs	HS	Avge	100	50
121	182	12	8540	291	50.23	24	45

Fielding:
    122 catches

Post script:

1) At Taunton in 1987, Glamorgan's fast bowler, Greg Thomas, smiled when he realised the wicket was to his liking. The Trebannws express fired in the first delivery causing Viv to back off sharply as the ball rose off a length. This prompted Greg to follow through and glare at the maestro and foolishly declare, 'It's red, it's round and it's fast – try hitting it.' Viv calmly ignored the comment, steadied himself and waited patiently for the next few deliveries. Two overs later, Viv stepped onto the back foot and viciously hooked a short ball into the River Tone. He stepped forward, prodded the crease, looked at Greg in the face whilst adding, 'Well, man. You know what it looks like; now go and get it.'

2) Viv Richards holds the record of most test runs in a calendar year – 1710 runs at an average of 90.

3) First Round Nat West Bank Trophy at St Helen's.
   Glamorgan: 322-5 (Richards 162*)
   Oxfordshire: 191-5

60
The Grandstand

Mark Rothco, the well-known American artist, was recently commissioned to create some masterpieces to hang on the wall of one of the more exclusive restaurants in New York City. As the commission was worth $2.5million, he wanted to get everything just right, so Rothco decided that the best course of action would be to visit the eatery and get a feel of the ambience of the place.

He booked a table, took along a friend and settled down to enjoy his evening. The waiters were charming and attentive, the food and wine was faultless and when the time came to leave, the artist was in high spirits, full of ideas about what he would paint – and then the bill arrived! Rothco said later that he had seldom been so depressed by a culinary experience and that he almost fainted when he saw the enormousness of the sum he was asked to pay. He decided there and then that he would turn down the commission.

It was obvious that only a small minority of New Yorkers would be able to patronise such an establishment, and by the same token, only a few people would see and enjoy his work. If the ordinary man on the street was denied this pleasure, what would be the point in his spending months, if not years, on a creation that was seen by only a few.

The St Helen's ground at Swansea has never been a place for the select few. The 'new' grandstand, built around 1927 to ensure that international games were played in west Wales, was never destined to become an iconic architectural landmark. The designs were not those of a Frank Lloyd Wright or a Baron Victor Horta – it was typically a utilitarian construction. Built entirely of wood, the grandstand stretched for a hundred yards along the Swansea foreshore from one goal post to the other. It could seat up to 3,200 spectators, sheltering those inside from the sometimes adverse weather conditions which prevailed.

In the early years, it was only the middle classes who could afford a seat in the stand (with the working-class supporters standing on the terrace backing onto Brynmill). However, as time went on it became open to all and, indeed, when the miners from the valleys, or those who worked in the copper quarter at Landore, were given a pay rise or bonuses at work, this was inevitably used to get a seat in the stand.

In this age of health and safety, perhaps it is fortuitous that the grandstand at St Helen's did not suffer the same fate as that of Bradford City's ground, the Valley, which was destroyed by fire in 1985 with 56 supporters losing their lives and 250 others being badly injured. One can imagine how a present-day fire officer would react to seeing over three thousand people crammed into a wooden structure, and with over half of them smoking cigarettes throughout the proceedings.

If the grandstand provided an excellent position from which to view a game of rugby, it was also a good place to watch cricket. I swear that if you sat in a particular seat you could see which way the ball spun, especially when Don Shepherd was bowling!

The viewing facilities from the stand might have been good, but the changing rooms and facilities underneath it were dire. The size of these rooms was about the same as a standard kitchen in any of the terrace houses overlooking the ground. It is said that the Swansea committee men were in a state of panic when the International Rugby Board ruled that there would be seven players on the substitutes bench – where would they change?

Things were no better for officials. I remember as a young boy visiting St Helen's wondering what it would be like to be allowed into the inner sanctum. On the first occasion I officiated there as a referee, I was about to find out. As I opened the door, I immediately crashed into the clothes hook on the adjacent wall. There was no room to swing the proverbial cat. Imagine the scene when there were three in there – the referee and two touch judges.

A grandstand of memories is all that remains.

Mike Cuddy's machines move in.

If conditions were a little archaic for the players and officials, they were no better for the press corps upstairs. If you worked for television, then you took your life in your hands as you had to straddle a beam under the eaves to get to the commentary position. The radio presenters did not fare any better – they were perched on planks of wood behind the last row of spectators. I always found sitting on a pile of books useful so that at least you could catch a glimpse of the game. We certainly weren't popular with those who sat in front of us as they complained bitterly that our constant chattering spoiled their enjoyment of the match!

It may have looked old and fragile from the day it was built, but the grandstand at St Helen's has served the community well for nearly eighty years. Until fairly recently it was a common sight to see the orderly queue snake its way back from the turnstiles towards the Patti Pavilion or Singleton Park. There was the air of excitement which followed once you had paid for your ticket and mounted the rickety staircase. The anticipation of finding your seat. You hoped against hope that you were not seated right up at the back in one of the corners, otherwise a pair of powerful binoculars was essential – but felt quite smug if you were anywhere near the halfway line.

When the whole structure was demolished a couple of seasons ago, there was no sound of wailing and gnashing of teeth when Mike Cuddy's machines moved in. As the Welsh Folk Museum ar St Fagan's had shown no interest in its reconstruction, the whole lot ended up on a rubbish tip.

While I have many fond memories of the grandstand and the environs, there is one occasion which I still find excruciatingly embarrassing to recall. Now if there was a league table of terrible performances by a rugby referee then I would surely be near the top after a match played at St Helen's in October 1974. The visitors were Pontypool and it was obvious from the kick off that the young referee wanted to exert his authority on the game. To this end, the

205

The ever-reliable Eddie Burns, a former player who still helps out on a voluntary basis.

PLAYERS, COMMITTEE & V.I.P.'S ONLY

whistle was blown at every opportunity, to the detriment of a flowing game and to the obvious frustration of the players involved. This feeling eventually overflowed onto the terraces and the grandstand so that, all in all, the game proved to be a disaster for all concerned.

Minutes after the final whistle, in the sanctuary of the referee's changing room, and with me contemplating immediate retirement, the door suddenly flew open. Standing in the doorway was Ieuan Evans, the Swansea coach. 'That is the worst display of refereeing I have ever seen,' he bellowed. 'If that's the best you can do, don't ever come here again.' With that, he turned on his heel and slammed the door shut. While I dried off after the longest shower taken to date, I contemplated Ieuan's words, and wondered how I could quietly slip out of St Helen's unnoticed – a boat to Ilfracombe perhaps!

As I emerged from the dressing room, who should be standing outside but the Swansea coach. He insisted that I accompany him to the clubhouse, all the while warding off the abuse (thankfully it was only vocal) from the home fans. That was Ieuan's way – he said what was on his mind, no more, no less and that was the end of the matter.

Amongst the many comments which came my way that afternoon, one was from a young female voice from the front row of the stand. Her booming voice was clearly heard by all – 'You should have stayed at the Odeon, referee.' These words were lost on me (and others present I might add) until I drove past the cinema on my back home. I saw the poster – Twiggy in *THE BOY FRIEND*. As a 6ft 4ins very thin individual, I saw her point and suddenly saw a new career looming! There was never a dull moment at St Helen's!

A dramatic silhouette of demolition.

61
Sarah Hopkins @ St Helen's

1986:

A native of mid-Glamorgan, the artist Sarah Hopkins has discovered an Aladdin's Cave in and around the city of Swansea. Such is the wealth of material available that Sarah has decided that the focus of her artistic skills will be the urban and industrial landscape of the area. One could say that girders, concrete façades, giant cranes, high-rise buildings, terraced houses, polluted landscapes, chimney stacks, satellite dishes, cobbled streets, and telegraph poles provide regular inspiration for the artist. 'Through the exploration of printmaking techniques, I endeavour to transform the monolithic monstrosities that blot our landscape into everyday beauty; a beauty, which in its wonderful and bizarre quirkiness is an integral part of my neighbourhood.'

2001:

For several years Sarah had travelled up and down the Mumbles Road, which borders St Helen's, on her way to and from work. On an almost daily basis, she had been sitting in her car gazing into the empty campus while she waited for pedestrians to use the crossing outside the main gate. With the eye of the artist, she marvelled at the intricate patterns created by the pillars supporting the floodlights, the shadows cast by the stands etc. However, she had only briefly set foot on the other side of the concrete wall.

The answer was to make an appointment to have a tour of the ground. With her young son Rhodri in tow, she spent a magical couple of hours sketching the outline of the pavilion, the old stand with its peeling paintwork, all a wealth of material for the discerning eye. Not to be outdone, the six-year-old Rhodri also added his contributions to the future masterpiece.

2002:

Lowri and Dafydd, our daughter and son-in-law, having just moved into their first marital home, were eager to buy some artwork to adorn the walls of their house in Creigiau near Llantrisant. To my amazement, the first thing that greeted me as I went through into the sitting room was a large screen print of St Helen's given pride of place above the fireplace. Having visited the Attic Gallery in Swansea, Lowri had fallen in love with the picture because it reminded her of all the happy hours we as a family had spent watching rugby and cricket at the ground.

From the time she had been pushed around the boundary in her pram, to the times she was dragged along in her teens, to the latter years when she voluntarily queued for her ticket at the turnstile, the place holds some special memories.

After meeting Sarah Hopkins in person, I was really rather pleased that a piece of art created by mother and son one sunny afternoon was now hanging in my own daughter's home.

P.S. Sarah obtained an MA in Fine Art with distinction at Swansea Institute in 2003 and is now a full-time lecturer at Gorseinon College.

62
The Greatest Ever Glamorgan XI

Is this the greatest ever Glamorgan XI? Undoubtedly the list will lead to heated discussions, with some supporters wishing to delete one or two names (possibly more) and adding some other outstanding Welsh cricketers. Please note, I haven't included any overseas players. The team selected will play the match at St Helen's which explains why I have nominated three (if not four) spin bowlers:

1 Alan JONES
2 Gilbert PARKHOUSE
3 Tony LEWIS (captain)
4 Matthew MAYNARD
5 Allan WATKINS
6 Peter WALKER
7 Jim PRESSDEE
8 Eifion JONES
9 Malcolm NASH
10 Don SHEPHERD
11 Steve WATKIN

And the opponents? Well what about the next best team – an XI captained by the irrepressible Wilf WOOLLER. I'm sure the team listed below could well cause an upset!

1 Hugh MORRIS
2 Emrys DAVIES
3 Steve JAMES
4 Maurice TURNBULL
5 Anthony COTTEY
6 H.G. DAVIES
7 Robert CROFT
8 Len MUNCER
9 Jim McCONNON
10 Wilfred WOOLLER (captain)
11 Jeff JONES

12th man: Adrian DALE

63
And the Best Swansea XV Ever?

It's only a personal choice, and I'm sure its publication will cause many arguments in the Swansea area. You don't have to agree!

15 W.J. Bancroft

14 Billy TREW
13 Scott GIBBS
12 Claude DAVEY
11 Dewi BEBB

10 W.T.H. (Willie) DAVIES
 9 R.M. (Dickie) OWEN

 1 W.O. WILLIAMS
 2 Garin JENKINS
 3 David YOUNG

 4 Geoff WHEEL
 5 Richard MORIARTY

 6 Colin CHARVIS
 8 Mervyn DAVIES
 7 Clem THOMAS

Acknowledgements

Sincere thanks to:
- my wife Jill for casting an eagle-eye on each chapter.
- Gomer Press for the invitation to compile this volume.
- David Price, Eddie Burns, Stuart Davies, Gethin Thomas, Les Williams, Mathew Powell, Heddyr Gregory, Staff at Swansea Library, Dr Andrew Hignell, Trystan Bevan, Edward Bevan, Rob Lloyd, The Right Honourable Peter Hain MP, Robert Gate, Guto Davies, Jane Wyn, Bleddyn Jones, Jim Mills, Delyth Owen, David Protheroe, Rob Lloyd.

Picture Acknowledgements

Huw Evans Picture Agency
Glamorgan County Cricket Club
John Harris
James Davies
David Jones
The South Wales Evening Post
The Phil Clift Collection
The Peter Davies Collection
The Eddie Burns Collection
D. Brian Davies, Pentyrch
Rebecca Storch, Pontyberem
Sarah Hopkins, Swansea
Swansea Military and Antiquarian Society
BBC Library
Colorsport

Every effort has been made to contact the copyright holders of all the pictures in this book. Gomer Press would be only too glad to receive any information about pictures whose sources we have been unable to credit.